PRAISE I

WALLPAPER WORSHIP

"Danny Byram helps us to understand the necessity of being spiritually alive and thoroughly committed to worship, which begins with God and His glory rather than with ourselves and our preferences. *Wallpaper Worship* is biblical, practical, and a vital resource for congregations and for those who lead them."

—Alistair Begg
Senior Minister, Parkside Church, Chagrin Falls, OH

"Whenever I am speaking at a conference, I am always delighted when Danny is leading the worship. Not only is he a gifted musician, but he understands worship. And, he understands how to help other people worship. This book gleans from his extensive international ministry and years of teaching. It will make you think. It will also make you want to worship like you never have before."

—Richard Blackaby
Author of *Living Out of the Overflow* and *The Seasons of God*
President, Blackaby Ministries International

"In *Wallpaper Worship*, Danny Byram defuses all the pointless dichotomies that so many books on worship get lost on. He gets to the core issues as only someone who has been involved for decades in shaping worship services, both great and small, could do. This book is not about changing our methods, but how our hearts can be changed by shifting priorities and focus, and by learning to truly care for those who find themselves simply showing up and lining the walls during worship."

—Michael Card
Writer, teacher, songwriter

WALLPAPER WORSHIP

WALLPAPER WORSHIP

WHY CHURCH MUSIC SOUNDS BETTER, FEWER
ARE SINGING, AND WHAT TO DO ABOUT IT

DANNY BYRAM

PUBLICATIONS

Fort Washington, PA 19034

Wallpaper Worship
Published by CLC Publications

U.S.A.
P.O. Box 1449, Fort Washington, PA 19034

UNITED KINGDOM
CLC International (UK)
Unit 5, Glendale Avenue, Sandycroft, Flintshire, CH5 2QP

Printed in the United States of America

ISBN (paperback): 978-1-61958-290-3
ISBN (e-book): 978-1-61958-291-0

Cover design by Mitch Bolton.

ACKNOWLEDGMENTS

When I was first asked to teach on the subject of worship, I was a bit stumped. At the time, it seemed easier to just lead worship than to articulate the whys and hows of worship. That was 1999, and since then there have been over two decades of workshops and conferences around the world.

As a young boy in love with music, and under the observation of my parents' ministry, I pursued a degree in sacred music. Yet it has been the last thirty plus years of my itinerant music/teaching ministry and event production that has given me the experience and knowledge base from which to write this book. The acknowledgments that follow reflect those who have invested in me and who share the message in these pages.

My wife, Angela, deserves the first acknowledgment for being the one who has emboldened me to be a man of integrity and selflessness, which is a challenge for someone who has lived his life on the platform to the accolades of many. Angela, you are truly the "wind beneath my wings." I enjoy the privilege of having a marriage, a family, and a ministry because of your patience, love, and sheer commitment to our partnership, and to the work God has called us to do together.

It is appropriate for me to acknowledge the shoulders this book stands on: My dad, Air Force Chaplain David Paul Byram, whom I watched and heard from his pulpits and desks in air force chapels. He taught me the importance of critical thinking. My mom, Nancy Byram, was my earliest musical influence. She was the one who modeled how to use music to lead congregants, choirs, and individuals into meaningful worship experiences, whether contemporary or traditional. A stickler for professional presentation, her heart was foremost for the participation of the worshippers she led.

More recently, I want to thank Lisa and Larry Cardenas for their encouragement to finish this project, even before we had a publisher. Lisa especially deserves a big thanks for proofing my premanuscript, which eventually became a real manuscript for CLC Publications. Thanks to my nephew Adrian Viccellio, for critiquing and editing my book proposal; and to Dave Almack, former publisher at CLC, who accepted the proposal because he shared a vision for what this book had to say. Janelle Harris, who edited and encouraged my revisions, deserves a big thanks for making my message clear, credible, and actually printable. Thanks also to Erika Cobb, managing editor for CLC, who talked with me like a summer camp counselor throughout the process.

I want to thank the prayer partners and financial friends of Danny Byram Ministries who have faithfully walked this journey alongside Angela and me for thirty years.

Finally, a heartfelt thanks to our children, who are all adults now, and who all follow and worship the triune Christian God: Father, Son, and Holy Spirit. Their confidence, encouragement, and advice lodges deeply into my soul. This book is an investment in their generation and the one to follow—the next historic cycle of worshippers who will worship in spirit and truth.

CONTENTS

PREFACE

WHAT IS WALLPAPER WORSHIP?

My earliest experiences in church music and Protestant worship were in US Air Force chapels. My father was a trained Southern Baptist minister who became an active-duty air force chaplain when I was in first grade. Every three years, we were moved to a new duty station. We started out at Loring Air Force Base (AFB) in Maine. From there we moved to Spangdahlem AFB in Germany, then to Altus AFB in Oklahoma, Mountain Home AFB in Idaho, and the US Air Force Academy in Colorado Springs.

There was usually a Catholic priest and five or six chaplains from various Protestant denominations at each base, and Dad served as one of those many chaplains while my mother assumed the role of the choir director at the base chapel. This was where my earliest musical training was cultivated. I started piano lessons in second grade at Loring AFB. I taught myself to play guitar and ukulele in fourth grade at Spangdahlem AFB. I was entered into piano competitions in junior high and sang pop songs with my guitar in school assemblies and musical theater productions at Altus AFB. In my senior year, I sang the bass solos in Handel's *Messiah* and took piano lessons at Mountain Home AFB from a teacher who had been a concert pianist at a music conservatory in Athens, Greece. I also landed my first professional singing job there. I was the music entertainment at a local restaurant for three hours every Friday and Saturday night, which helped me save money for college. When I started, my dad asked if I had enough songs to last a weekend, so I made a list of all the songs I knew. I stopped at 375. I could've sung every weekend for months without one repeat. By that time, it was obvious to me, my family, and my friends that I was going to be a music major. So I left Mountain Home AFB for Oral Roberts University in Tulsa, Oklahoma and started my undergrad studies.

While I was earning my bachelor of music degree in sacred music, I performed in pizza restaurants, hotel lounges, churches, the Elks lodge—anywhere someone invited me to provide entertainment. Sacred music and hymnology seemed like a weird specialty to me since most of my time was spent doing music that wasn't sacred and my performances weren't inside church buildings. As much as I appreciated my classical-based training by day, I really wanted to grab my guitar and head to Nashville, Music City USA, to write songs and become a recording artist.

In the last semester of my senior year, a Nashville-based recording artist named Gene Cotton performed on campus. He wasn't a huge star, but I'd heard a couple of his songs on the radio and I was curious enough to attend his concert. Since I knew the students in charge of the event, I was able to get backstage to chat with him. I explained that while I was earning my music degree, I was singing in churches, clubs, and restaurants around town trying to build a fan base. Some of my admirers were encouraging me to go to Las Vegas and perform in the casinos. Cotton looked at me and said, "That's great advice if your dream is to be singing your heart out while people walk by and stare at you as they count their gambling chips. If you want to make wallpaper music, go to Las Vegas." I didn't want my music to be passively heard or completely ignored. So I took his advice. I never went to Las Vegas.

Wallpaper music isn't designed for serious listening or engagement. Like the wallpaper that hangs in a living room, it exists to enhance the design of the surroundings. No matter the skill or sincerity of the musicians who perform it, wallpaper music serves a passive purpose and requires little participation from its listeners. When we are shopping at the supermarket, we are accompanied by background music produced to make us feel good as we spend money. When I am dining at my favorite Mexican restaurant, I am audibly transported to that country by the mariachi music playing through the sound system. When we walk into a dentist's office, we are as nervous as an ant on a freeway until we are intentionally calmed by the soothing sounds of smooth jazz. Wallpaper music is pleasant to the ear but it does little for the spirit.

WALLPAPER MUSIC YIELDS WALLPAPER WORSHIP

My wife, Angela, and I were invited by friends to attend a worship service at one of the largest churches in the Denver area, where we live. After hearing about how different the experience of this church's worship style was for other people, we were curious: What new experience would we observe? We entered the main auditorium, a ten-thousand-seat arena with two-story-high video walls surrounding the stage and four stationary television cameras on floor platforms throughout the seats. The atmosphere was electric with anticipation. Suddenly, the house lights went down, the stage lights blinked, and the screens showed masterful camerawork by the video team. After taking their place on stage, the band began to play with precision and style. The musicians seemed to be very much engaged in what they were doing. I looked right, left, behind, and up to the balcony. About 80 percent of the people were visibly disengaged from what was happening on the stage. Some were chatting in small groups; some were nestled into the theater-style seats sipping coffee. Most of those present were merely standing on their feet watching the band play and sing. As sincere as the musicians seemed and as great as the music sounded, the people in the congregation were not connecting to the songs. It was painful to watch the musicians playing their hearts out, mouthing meaningful lyrics to a crowd that was, for the most part, paying them no attention. I thought to myself: *This looks just like Las Vegas.*

Was this church different? From what I have witnessed as I travel the nation and the world visiting churches, Christian conference centers, and military chapel services, churchgoers are experiencing this wallpaper worship in congregations as large as ten thousand or as small as one hundred. Many across the landscape of present-day church leadership say that this kind of nonparticipatory experience is what the current culture demands. As well meaning as that explanation is, it ignores the bigger picture. The issue is rooted in a fundamental point that what we have been calling worship may not be worship at all. The church has redefined worship to fit a cultural model instead of a biblical one, much to the ignorance of many newly churched believers and the dismay of mature worshippers who have been around long enough to know the difference. This redefinition has evolved from a well-intentioned desire to connect with the surrounding culture in a relevant, contemporary way. The challenge is to understand which components of worship we are compelled by the Scriptures to never change in a social culture that is constantly changing.

I do not believe that what we had in the church seventy years ago should be considered the "golden age of worship." As you will see in the pages ahead, wallpaper worship is not new. Early in its history, the church had eras of glorious worship followed by stumbles into passivity. Some of these periods lasted for hundreds of years until a groundswell movement helped the church find its voice again and begin to worship God in new ways that were alive in spirit and truth. If we fail to consider the historical context in which we inherited the practice of worship, we find ourselves vulnerable to repeating mistakes of the past, no matter how well we gift wrap those mistakes. I hope this book awakens our identity as corporate and individual worshippers and enlightens us about who we are: a privileged, powerful people who will not settle for passivity and passionately participate in all of our God-ordained activities, the first of which is worship.

—Danny Byram

INTRODUCTION

THIS IS A FOOTBALL

In 1959, Vince Lombardi became the new head coach of the Green Bay Packers. When he took the job, the team's record said it all—they were losers. Assuming they had a desire to win, even though they had won only two of twelve seasons, the new coach concluded what they had been doing wasn't leading them in a winning direction. It was up to him to earn their trust and lead them in a new direction. As he stood before them surveying their woebegone faces, he told his players that under his leadership, they were going to return to the fundamentals of the game. He picked up a football and gave what was to become the most famous quote in NFL history: "Gentlemen, . . . this is a football."[1]

Lombardi's simple point that day was likely met with reluctance and cynicism. But he knew something that his players had long forgotten. Leadership is about guiding followers to a desired goal. That season, the Packers followed their new coach on a journey that led them out of the loser's column to become NFL champions. It was a journey into the fundamentals of the game. It was a journey back to the basics.

HOW DID WE GET HERE?

Confronting the "Ghosts of Worship Past" helps to uncover how we arrived at this current state of corporate worship. As we understand our history of worship, we more clearly see our present worship. Inevitably, this kind of reflection forces the question: "Why are we doing what we are doing the way we are doing it?"

I believe we experience worship in cycles. Before the Reformation of the sixteenth century, those cycles turned slowly over several hundred years. In my lifetime alone, there have been movements and cycles that have changed how the church approaches its worship practices. From 1962–1965, the Catholic Church changed many of its centuries-old practices of worship through the ecumenical council referred to as Vatican II. One of those changes no longer required the Mass to be recited in Latin. Instead, it was spoken in vernacular language. Folk music styles were also incorporated into worship and used as liturgical music. The result was the folk mass, which became a precursor to the contemporized music in the Protestant traditions. By 1969, four years after Vatican II, the Jesus movement started in Southern California. It changed not only the style of Protestant worship, but created churches that are still leading the contemporary worship movement into the twenty-first century. There have been other movements before and since: the Great Awakenings, the D.L. Moody Crusades, the

Billy Graham Crusades, Promise Keepers. Even with a simple cursory observation over my own lifetime, one can reach the conclusion that we tend to experience worship cycles not every few hundred years as in ancient times, but every fifty to seventy years and now as quickly as twenty-five to thirty years.

Since societal change is faster now, the cycles are shorter, starting and restarting before one generation has moved on. As we examine these cycles, it may be surprising to see where we are now in the early portion of the twenty-first century. A new normal has been established in the Western church. It has very little relation to whether rock music or traditional hymns are used in worship services. It does not matter whether your church uses a rhythm section or a pipe organ. It has nothing to do with liturgical elements or if a church meets in a remodeled bowling alley or a five hundred-year-old cathedral. The new normal is this: Many of our worship gatherings have become passive activities that often are akin to attending a motivational seminar, a ticketed concert, or watching a TV reality show. Those provide a vicarious experience for the viewer. The downbeat is hit, the program begins, the adrenaline starts, and suddenly we become observers transported into someone else's world. Many churchgoers in today's church market are experiencing worship in a similar way. Are we designing and executing our services to encourage passive observation? Do we think this is what congregants want? More importantly, is this what they need?

WHY THIS BOOK?

As someone who has led, performed, preached, and produced in NFL stadiums and NBA arenas, makeshift chapels and US combat zones, I can attest—as many others can—that real worship is participatory. It has little to do with the location of the service, size of the crowd, comfort of culture, style of music, availability of gear, or whether the latest songs are used.

This book is the core curriculum of what I have taught in my worship workshops around the world since 1999. Getting back to the fundamentals of biblical Christian worship will help us to achieve corporate worship experiences that are fully participatory and spiritually powerful. In my touring and teaching over the past thirty years as a musician and minister, I have observed believers genuinely excited about worship as they understand it. What birthed the curriculum of my worship workshops was the lack of understanding of a biblical perspective on worship in contemporary, traditional, and even liturgical contexts.

There is an old phrase that parodies the Seven Last Words of Christ. It is called the Seven Last Words of the Church and they are: We've never done it this way before. Whether you are a leader, elder, deacon, pastor, musician, or lay volunteer, you may get excited about designing a new game plan and what it could mean for the people you lead and serve. You may get a vision of what is possible at a deeper level in your own life as a worshipper. I have learned in my own work as a leader, both in my ministry and in my marriage and family, that a good leader is wise. I have also learned to never act in isolation or reaction. As you read this book, share it with others in your community and see if they resonate with what is being put forward here. Remember, change is difficult.

For Coach Lombardi, the destination was simple: Get the team to carry the ball over the goal line. They had the uniforms, the equipment, the facilities, and the talent, but they were not reaching the goal. What they lacked was a leader who understood how to create a new game plan that would harness their assets to lead the team to where they ultimately wanted to be. This book is about harnessing assets that belong exclusively to the church for the purpose of leading people into a powerful worship experience that is fully participatory, transforming, and powerful, regardless of the style, size, culture, or location. If your game plan isn't working, it's time to scrap it and get back to the basics of what worship is—and is not—and what it can be. So, ladies and gentlemen, "This is a football."

1

WORSHIP: A MAJOR AWARD

The perfect church service would be the one
we were almost unaware of; our attention would have been on
God. But every novelty prevents this.

—C.S. Lewis

Our family has a list of movies that have become "the Byram classics." No matter how many times we watch them, they guarantee laughs for us and our guests. One of those movies is *A Christmas Story*,[1] which follows the school and home misadventures of a ten-year-old boy named Ralphie during the holiday season in 1948 Indiana. Narrated by his adult self, the film marks Ralphie's dreams of getting a BB gun for Christmas and the hints he drops to his distracted parents.

One scene that is central to the story's comedy is when Ralphie's dad (the "old man") arrives home from work announcing he has won "a major award" from a crossword puzzle contest and that it will arrive sometime that evening.

Later, as the family is having dinner, there is a knock at the door. They rush from the table and watch with anticipation as a large wooden crate is delivered. The old man manically pries open the wooden cover. And as he dives into the crate, sending packing materials flying, he lifts out his "major award": a lamp that is a replica of a woman's leg, complete with a shade on top that looks like it came from an 1890s saloon.

Young Ralphie's eyes bug out. His younger brother Randy's mouth drops open. Their mother is horrified as she covers Randy's eyes. But the old man's face glows with pride and excitement. It doesn't matter to him what it looks like; it's his major award! He quickly moves furniture, carefully positions the leg lamp in the front room window, plugs it in, and runs outside to admire the glow of his prize from the sidewalk. Just then a neighbor walks up slowly, staring in confusion. The neighbor asks the old man what that thing is in the window. The old man proudly announces that it is a major award. The neighbor squints his eyes and responds sheepishly, as if to say, *Really? It looks like a lamp to me.*

Since the word *worship* evokes images and meanings that were not linked to it as recently as a few decades ago, it's easy to find ourselves staring at something in a church service that looks and sounds familiar, but is not completely recognizable. The people on stage are closing their eyes and are engaged in some kind of worshipful expression. If perchance the live sound is mixed favoring the vocalists, you might understand a few scriptural phrases. But why are so many congregation members leaving these religious gatherings feeling as if they missed something? They sound good. They sound right. We are told they are worship experiences. They are billed as worship experiences. Yet I often hear reactions similar to the neighbor squinting and viewing the leg lamp in the window. "What is that?" a congregant asks. The reply: "It's worship." The response: "Really?"

WORSHIP REDEFINED

The American version of English has a reputation of being non-English English. That's no more evident—and frustrating—than when you travel to London and need to find a restroom. To the English, you are looking for *the loo*. As Professor Henry Higgins sings in the musical theater classic, *My Fair Lady*: "There even are places where English completely disappears. In America, they haven't used it for years!"[2] He's quite right. Even words in our common language can have very different meanings. Over time, vernacular language becomes tired and submits to colloquialism.

Another reason words or phrases receive new and adjusted meanings are because the new meaning can serve a larger purpose when the populace catches on. Here are some examples:

WORD	OLD MEANING	NEW MEANING
Green	A color	Environmentally safe or friendly
Embezzlement	A crime of stealing	Misappropriation of funds
Gay	A jovial mood	Homosexual
Stream	A flow of water	A flow of electronic information
Thread	Used to sew on a button	A flow of electronic conversation
It	The old man's major award	A gaudy leg lamp

Webster's American English Dictionary offers a concise definition of the word *worship*: "devotion to a deity." It's pretty simple and easy to understand. Yet worship has been redefined by our current Christian culture. I first heard the word used in the songwriting context in the late 1980s when a company called Hosanna! Integrity (now Integrity Inc.) began to publish and release cassette recordings of the musical portions of worship services. Because of their simple choruses, those short, repetitive songs had been previously known in the 1970s as "praise choruses" and eventually became familiar to listeners and musicians as "worship songs" because they were easy to follow, perform, and use in participative group singing. The song form itself has roots much further back than the 1980s.[3] Over time, the usage of the music came with a new usage of the word *worship*. When I was recording in Nashville in the early 1990s, the song style had become accepted and known as simply "praise and worship." At one of my recording sessions, some of the studio musicians I hired to assist me asked, "Is your music P&W?"

There are unspoken rules behind the current usage and meaning of the word *worship*. Inherent to those rules is the assumption that anyone without that knowledge is out of touch.

Worship is a gathering of Christian people.
Worship is the programmed flow of a service.
Worship is the music portion of the service.
Worship is a style of music.
Worship is a song form within a style of music.
Worship is a lifestyle.
Worship is an emotion.

CONSIDER THE FOLLOWING EXAMPLES OF CURRENT WORSHIP PHRASEOLOGY.

"Are you doing worship?"	This question is generally directed to (a) a person planning to attend a worship service or (b) a musician invited to play music in a church service.
"When will we sing worship songs?"	This makes the distinction between hymns, instrumentals, and other styles.
"You'll do the worship portion of the service."	A musician is being given instruction that their music will be played during segments in the service designated for music only, particularly group singing.
"Make sure you do some praise and worship."	The phrase "praise and worship" denotes a specific song form or repertoire, anything but a hymn or a solo piece.
"We loved your worship."	A compliment I have personally received over the years. It means "we liked your song selections, the way you performed them, or the way we felt when you performed them."
"Did you like that worship?"	This is asked to determine if a person liked or disliked a set of songs (or a solo) used in a service. It is also a litmus test for judging a congregation's musical taste.
"Girl, you worship!"	A compliment directed to a friend who demonstratively participated in a worship service.

Some may quip, "I see. Sometimes, it's simply about using the word *worship* in place of the word *music*. What's the big deal?" Oh, if it were that simple. There are at least a dozen possible ways *worship* can be used in the above examples. All of them create nuances that may or may not be consistent with each other. In other words, you may choose to scramble, fry, poach, or throw an egg, but it is always an egg. Not so with worship. This diversity of use and nuance is risky because:

1. It fails to ensure what is being transmitted or what is being received.
2. The interpretation is completely subjective to the moment, the context, or the culture.
3. The new meaning of the word may not line up with the biblical meaning of the word.

A pastor I worked with for a number of years had a flashy and dramatic style of communication. Congregants were thrilled as he used movie clips and dramatic soliloquies to illustrate his points and entertain his audience. But if you asked congregants as they were leaving the service, you would find that few understood what he was actually talking about. When asked, "What was the point he was making?" I heard the response: "I have no idea, but it sounded great!" In other words, it's plugged in and it's glowing in the window. But what is it?

WHAT'S SO AMAZING ABOUT WORSHIP?

What is truly amazing about our Christian worship heritage is the vast array of styles, colors, music, art, liturgies, and improvisations in the spirit. As a people group, Christians have inherited an incredibly colorful history of worship expressions. There are places today where many of these tools are being used in creative ways to capture the hearts and minds of those in attendance and connect them with the truth of the gospel. For instance, Angela and I recently attended a "night of worship" at a nearby church where music was performed; liturgical readings, poetry, and Scripture passages were shared; and testimonies were given. Meanwhile, visual artists were at work around the room, creating paintings and interpreting in art what was being communicated from the platform. Though this kind of experience in a worship service setting may not happen every week, going to a worship service should be something we find incredibly rich to our minds and hearts.

Regardless of style, any worship service that is boring and predictable is like going to an art museum with paintings that are all blue. After moving through two or three galleries, one may ask, "Is this it? Why aren't there any paintings in other colors?" After seeing every exhibit in one color, we may get so used to it that we begin to think, "Well, I guess this is art." The same mistake can be made in our worship habits. When few congregants are participating—standing around drinking coffee, chatting, or passively observing the goings on from the platform—we can get so used to it that we may walk away thinking, "Well, I guess this is worship." Perhaps we should ask a tougher question: Is what we are calling worship boring and predictable?

Our son, Jeremy, and his wife, Carly, have volunteered at their church to help with music and sound. One Sunday, he was stationed in the rear of the sanctuary helping with lyric projection when one of the pastors decided to stand in the back with him during that particular service. Normally, the pastors dutifully sit on the front row. The service opens with church announcements followed by the opening set of music. When the band took its place on the platform and started to play, one third of the congregants made their way to the aisles, through the doors, and into the lobby for coffee and visiting. The pastor turned to Jeremy and asked, "What's happening? Why is everyone leaving?" He was completely unaware that what he was observing had been happening every Sunday behind his back. Oddly, no one who was leading from the platform and facing the congregation ever brought it up in a planning meeting. Hmm.

So why are they leaving? Why are so few singing and so many standing around observing, as if they're waiting for something else to happen? The answer is obvious to those willing to consider it: There's not much there demanding people's participation. How can that be, we ask? We have rehearsed our heads off. We have all the right gear and talent to create the sound of world-class praise and worship.

The same phenomenon is true for nonmusical portions of a worship service. A speaker may think, I have worked so hard on this sermon and no one seems to get it. What's wrong with these people? But is it really the congregation's fault? More and more churchgoers are starting to realize that their worship experience may be something other than a worship experience. It may contain elements of music, a teaching, some movie clips, a dramatic characterization, and definitely a bunch of announcements. But what is it?

The *Washington Post* published an editorial by a millennial reflecting on her church experience. In it, she said, "The trick isn't to make church cool, it's to keep worship weird. You can get a cup of coffee with your friends anywhere, but church is the only place you can get ashes smudged on your forehead as a reminder of your mortality. You can be dazzled by a light show at a concert on any given weekend, but church is the only place that fills a sanctuary with candlelight and hymns on Christmas Eve."[4]

AN OBSERVER'S SPORT

Wallpaper worship is an observer's sport and since watching reality TV, clicking YouTube links, and streaming video on our phones and laptops is the cultural norm, doing worship as an anonymous nonparticipant feels somewhat normal. However, when there is little, if any, participation, it doesn't take long for congregants to realize they are actually just passive observers, providing a weekly audience for a group of performers.

Are we bound to this kind of experience simply because we happen to live in an era of passivity and vicarious media experiences? Is there more to this worship thing than what we are getting? Is a nonparticipatory observance of a performance what the Father intended for His worshippers? When we gather to sing, pray, recite, take sacraments, listen to a Bible teaching, sing again, and depart, do we do so with a sense that something extraordinary has happened in our midst? Or have we settled for a rational, linear, television program-like experience because that is what we are used to?

OK, SO WHAT IS WORSHIP?

Getting back to the fundamentals requires us to agree on what worship is and what worship isn't. To get clarity, why don't we find out what the Bible has to say on worship? Let's look at one of the shortest yet most revealing passages that

gives us the purpose, characteristics, and results of worship—
the five verses of Psalm 100.

> Make a joyful noise to the LORD, all the earth!
> > Serve the LORD with gladness!
> > Come into his presence with singing!
>
> Know that the LORD, he is God!
> > It is he who made us, and we are his;
> > we are his people, and the sheep of his pasture.
>
> Enter his gates with thanksgiving,
> > and his courts with praise!
> > Give thanks to him; bless his name!
>
> For the LORD is good;
> > his steadfast love endures forever,
> > and his faithfulness to all generations.

THE PURPOSE OF WORSHIP

Worship causes humility. When we "come into his presence with singing" (100:2), something profound becomes obvious: He is God and we are not. It is humbling to realize "we are his people, the sheep of his pasture" (100:3). Think about it. This Lord, who is God Himself, has created His own people. That's us! This is a humbling thought in our world of self-made, rugged individualism.

Worship honors His power, His praise, and His plan. Our humility in worship causes us to declare God's power, not our own. It also verbalizes His praise. Verse 4 says that thanksgiving and praise is the posture with which we enter the place of worship: "Give thanks to him; bless his name!" Worship also declares that His love is everlasting for all people of the past, present, and future: "For the LORD is good; his steadfast love endures forever, and his faithfulness to all generations" (Ps. 100:5). Worship makes us humble so we can declare His power, praise, and plan to "all the earth" (100:1).

The more we worship, the more humble we become. The more humble we become, the easier it is to declare His power, His praise, and His plan. This is the purpose of worship.

THE CHARACTERISTICS OF WORSHIP

Worship is corporate. Verses 1, 2, and the opening line of verse 3 all use the imperative commands of make, serve, come, know. The implied subject of the commands is "*you* make, *you* serve, *you* come, *you* know." That this is a plural *you* becomes clearer as we move into verse 3 and beyond: "It is he who made us, and we are his; we are his people." It doesn't say "it is he who made me" or "I am his person." This psalm talks of worship as being a corporate activity with the participation of many.

Worship is private. It is clear from other passages besides Psalm 100 that worship can also be a private activity—involving prayer (see Matt. 6:6), fasting (see 6:16), offerings (see 6:4), and praise through song or prose (Hannah's prayer of praise in First Samuel 2:1–10 or Mary's Magnificat in Luke 1:46–55).

The Bible is clear that the characteristics of worship are not corporate *or* private. Rather, worship is both corporate *and* private.

THE RESULTS OF WORSHIP

Worship results in grief over our sin. This kind of godly grief or sorrow (as seen in Second Corinthians 7:9) is a fruit of the humility it takes in knowing "that the LORD, he is God! It is he who made us, and we are his" (Ps. 100:3). Every worship experience does not necessarily lead to grieving over sin, but it is worth recognizing this as one result of worshipping a holy God.

When the nation of Israel returned to Jerusalem after being held captive in Babylon for seventy long years, their governor, Nehemiah, and the priest, Ezra, called for an assembly. There was a celebration wherein Ezra read the Law of God for seven days. In describing the event, Nehemiah 8:9 says, "For all the people wept as they heard the words of the Law." In Nehemiah 9:1–3, they wept in humility, realizing how they and their ancestors had been disobedient. Then "they stood up in their place and read from the Book of the Law of the LORD their God for a quarter of the day; for another quarter of it they made confession [of their sin] and worshiped the LORD their God" (9:3). The rest of chapter 9 is their declaration of not only their sin but also God's power, praises, and plans for them.

Worship results in joy over God's forgiveness and loving-kindness. Psalm 100:4 tells us to "bless his name!" Why should we bless His name? Verse 5 elaborates: "his steadfast love endures forever, and his faithfulness to all generations."

Again, Nehemiah said something very similar to the people of Israel when they wept over their sin: " 'This day is holy to the LORD your God; do not mourn or weep.' For all the people wept as they heard the words of the Law. Then he said to them, 'Go your way. Eat the fat and drink sweet wine and send portions to anyone who has nothing ready, for this day is holy to our Lord. And do not be grieved, for the joy of the LORD is your strength' " (Neh. 8:9–10). Sounds like a great worship service, which ended in joy.

Worship results in unity of direction. When we declare God's plans, there is always action to be taken for us to fulfill them. God's people come together in one heart and mind to do His will. Psalm 100 is five verses of commands, not only for corporate and personal worship, but also for living life itself: make, serve, come, know, enter, give, bless. These are the ways we not only worship in a gathering, but also worship with our lives—in the doing of life—as a community of believers and followers of God, reaching out to our neighbors and the world around us in the name of Jesus Christ.

As we move forward, drilling further down into the details inside of worship, let's start with the Son of God Himself and His report of what His Father in heaven's view is on worship.

2

THE WORSHIP CONVERSATION

*"Come now, let us reason together," says the L*ORD.

Isaiah 1:18

THE WORSHIP CONVERSATION OF JOHN 4

Even though the Bible does not define the word *worship*, the story in John 4 is the closest thing we have to an explanation of what it really is. The conversation between Jesus and an anonymous Samaritan woman at the well of Sychar is not only a great place to begin our understanding of worship, but shows us some clear similarities to where we are now. Before we launch into it, there are a few contextual ideas of which we must be aware.

The interaction between Jesus and the Samaritan woman in verses 7–26 is significant for a number of reasons. First, a strict first-century rabbi would have considered it morally risky to have such a theological and personal conversation with a woman other than his wife. In his book *Sacred Marriage*, Gary Thomas mentions the misogyny that was prevalent at the time: "Not only was it unheard of for a rabbi to be alone with a woman, but to discuss theology was virtually unthinkable. One rabbi, when it was suggested to him that women be taught the Law for particular circumstances, replied, 'If any man gives his daughter a knowledge of the Law it is as though he taught her lechery.'"[1] Jesus ignored that tradition. Following the private conversation, the disciples showed up at the well from their journey into the nearby town to fetch lunch and "marveled" that He was talking with a woman (see John 4:8, 27).

Second, the woman was not a Jew. She was from a tribe that was half Hebrew and half pagan.[2] Because of the mixing of breeds and faith, Jews considered Samaritans to be a lower and shamed class. Because of their prejudice, they journeyed for days to avoid even traveling through Samaria. So Jesus and His disciples' journey into the heart of Samaria was akin to taunting or picking a fight in the wrong part of town. It stands to reason that the disciples "marveled" at the trip altogether. It makes one wonder, given the prejudice of Jews against Samaritans, if any of the twelve disciples had ever been in Samaria prior to that trip.

Third, keep in mind as you read through this conversation that Jesus stated later in John 8:26: "He who sent me is true, and I declare to the world what I have heard from him." What Jesus said to the woman at the well was not something He made up on the spot. It is a mirror of the Father's heart, not only for a shamed, mixed-background, adulterous woman. Jesus' words are the Father's words for *all* who desire to hear them.

Finally, Jesus taught through parables in the Gospels. He often used the phrase "the kingdom of God is like . . ." and then provided relatable stories and analogies for His listeners.

After Jesus' telling of those parables, even His closest followers sometimes could not understand the point of His story and had to ask for clarification. Not so in this conversation. Jesus did not speak to the Samaritan woman through parable or story form, but directly relayed the Father's views on worship as He addressed her in a very personal and private situation. Let's read the story as it appears in John 4:5–26.

> So he came to a town of Samaria called Sychar, near the field that Jacob had given to his son Joseph. Jacob's well was there; so Jesus, wearied as he was from his journey, was sitting beside the well. It was about the sixth hour.
>
> A woman from Samaria came to draw water. Jesus said to her, "Give me a drink." (For his disciples had gone away into the city to buy food.) The Samaritan woman said to him, "How is it that you, a Jew, ask for a drink from me, a woman of Samaria?" (For Jews have no dealings with Samaritans.) Jesus answered her, "If you knew the gift of God, and who it is that is saying to you, 'Give me a drink,' you would have asked him, and he would have given you living water." The woman said to him, "Sir, you have nothing to draw water with, and the well is deep. Where do you get that living water? Are you greater than our father Jacob? He gave us the well and drank from it himself, as did his sons and his livestock." Jesus said to her, "Everyone who drinks of this water will be thirsty

again, but whoever drinks of the water that I will give him will never be thirsty again. The water that I will give him will become in him a spring of water welling up to eternal life." The woman said to him, "Sir, give me this water, so that I will not be thirsty or have to come here to draw water."

Jesus said to her, "Go, call your husband, and come here." The woman answered him, "I have no husband." Jesus said to her, "You are right in saying, 'I have no husband'; for you have had five husbands, and the one you now have is not your husband. What you have said is true." The woman said to him, "Sir, I perceive that you are a prophet. Our fathers worshiped on this mountain, but you say that in Jerusalem is the place where people ought to worship." Jesus said to her, "Woman, believe me, the hour is coming when neither on this mountain nor in Jerusalem will you worship the Father. You worship what you do not know; we worship what we know, for salvation is from the Jews. But the hour is coming, and is now here, when the true worshippers will worship the Father in spirit and truth, for the Father is seeking such people to worship him. God is spirit, and those who worship him must worship in spirit and truth." The woman said to him, "I know that Messiah is coming (he who is called Christ). When he comes, he will tell us all things." Jesus said to her, "I who speak to you am he."

OK, let's break this passage down into the style of a screen-play in order to experience the story.

Jesus is hot and tired, and He sits down at the well of Sychar while His disciples have gone into town to fetch supplies. He is sitting alone during lunch hour. Eventually a woman, walking alone, approaches to draw water.

JESUS. Hi there. Kinda hot today, isn't it? Can I get a drink of water from you?

WOMAN, *noticing that He is wearing traditional Jewish clothing with a marked Jewish woven shawl around His head and prayer tassels hanging from His outer garment.* Really? How is it that a Jewish man would talk to me, a Samaritan woman, much less ask me for a drink? What are You, some kind of practical joker?

JESUS. No, not a joker. But I am different. If you knew who I really am, you'd ask Me to give you some living water.

WOMAN, *sarcastically.* Living water, huh? Right. Well, tell me this, Mr. Jewish Joker. How are You gonna draw water when You don't even have anything to draw it out of the well with? (*Rolls her eyes.*) Are You some kind of Jewish big shot who thinks He's greater than our father Jacob, who gave us Samaritans this well?

(Remember, Jacob's name was changed to Israel in Genesis 32:28. Perhaps she is proud that she shares a heritage with this Jew or perhaps she is feeling the need to "one-up" Him and remind Him they come from similar stock.)

JESUS. Interesting that you mention that. But you know what? You'll never thirst again if you drink the living water I can give you. It will become like your own personal inner well, springing up forever. Sounds crazy, doesn't it? But it's true!

WOMAN, *putting down her bucket.* Well sure. I'd love something like that. Who wouldn't? Then I wouldn't have to come out here in the heat every day, hauling heavy buckets of water back to my house. OK, work your magic. I'll take this living water of Yours.

JESUS. Great. But first, go back home and bring your husband here with you.

WOMAN, *her face falling, showing hurt and anger.* I don't have a husband. (*Stands and grabs her bucket to resume getting water.*) I am nobody's wife!

JESUS. I know. You've had five husbands and the guy you're living with now isn't your husband. You have stated the truth, woman. I like your honesty. It's refreshing. Kind of a rare trait these days.

WOMAN, *feeling scared, she drops her bucket to the ground and water spills.* You're no joker. You're some kind of "prophet of God." How else could You know this about me?

JESUS, *gently.* Don't be scared. I'm not here to hurt you in any way. Please, sit down.

WOMAN, *slowly sitting down again on the side of the well.* You know, I'm kinda religious. I mean, I know that our forefathers used to worship at this mountain. But you Jews tell everybody it is not good enough to know that. You people seem so arrogant, always coming down on others unless they worship the way you do in Jerusalem. So if You're a holy man, what do You think about that?

JESUS, *with kindness.* My dear lady, you can believe me when I tell you that a time is coming when people will worship the Father of heaven neither here at your mountain nor even in Jerusalem. I know we Jews are a proud people, and rightly so, since the Father chose to bring salvation to the world through us. But guess what? The day is here when men, women, and children of all races and nations will worship the Father in spirit and in truth. He is looking for worshippers like that. You no longer have to do anything, follow old rules, come up with new forms, or go anywhere special to worship God. In fact, I came from Him—I hear His voice and He shows me His heart.

WOMAN, *after a long pause.* When I was a little girl, I heard stories about a Messiah, a Savior, who would come and tell us things like this. Is it true? Is it You?

JESUS, *looking into her eyes and smiling.* Yes. I am The One. It is Me. Do you believe Me?

WOMAN. I think I do … (*Stands to her feet.*) Yes, I know I do!

There are many key moments and points in this conversation. Let's look at a few and then we'll focus on what Jesus says to her about worship.

As stated earlier, the fact that Jesus revealed the Father's heart on worship to a *woman* reinforced a common message made clear through similar encounters in His short lifetime:

1. His inclusion of Mary Magdalene
2. His treatment of the woman with the issue of blood
3. The forgiveness He extended to the woman caught in adultery
4. The fact that it was women who found the empty tomb and were the first to report it to the male disciples (who were busy that Sunday morning hiding for their lives)

Those encounters with Jesus tore down a standard shared in Judaism and the world at large that women were to be undervalued, discredited, and used by men. Jesus completely blew that view apart during His ministry and demonstrated it in the intimate conversation with the Samaritan woman.

Jesus used Samaritans as examples of how Jews should behave—for example, the Good Samaritan who rescued a man being robbed and beaten on the road while Jewish leaders passed him by (see Luke 10:29–37) and the ten lepers in Luke 17:12 who were healed, nine of them Jews and one a Samaritan. Guess which one came back to thank Jesus for healing him? The Samaritan. We have to deduce that as a young boy growing up in Nazareth, Jesus was privy to the jokes and racial epithets Jews likely hurled at Samaritans. In John 8:48, Jesus' fellow Jews dishonored Him by saying, "Are we not right in saying that you are a Samaritan and have a demon?" Perhaps this is why Jesus used Samaritans as a teaching example. It probably infuriated many of His Jewish listeners.

REGARDING WORSHIP

Let's turn our focus now to what Jesus says to this woman regarding worship. He challenges patterns of thought that this woman had probably adopted in childhood. For reasons not revealed in this story, she believes that the geographical location of worship is important. Her Samaritan people say one thing (worship has to take place at Mount Gerizim near the well of Sychar); Jews say another (worship must take place exclusively in Jerusalem). Jesus tells her that location—as well as birthright, nationality, gender, and culture—is not important to God.

How many churches have split about differences on the topics of location, nationality, gender, culture, or personal preferences? The dogma of whichever group we belong to generally upholds that group as the practitioners of real worship. Jesus demolished that idea in one sentence: "Woman, believe me, the hour is coming when neither on this mountain nor in Jerusalem will you worship the Father" (John 4:21).

The concept of nonexclusivity regarding worship—how, where, or with whom it was done—is not new. The Old Testament is full of instances where God makes it clear that He will open up His blessings to all people. Yes, it is true that God started with the Jews. But it is evident that His plan was always to welcome strangers (see Deut. 10:19), forgive Nineveh (see Jon. 3:5–10), and seek and save the lost (see Luke 19:10). In Ezekiel 33:11, God is quoted by the prophet as saying, "I have no pleasure in the death of the wicked, but that the wicked turn from his way and live." God has always been seeking true worshippers who will worship Him in spirit and in truth.

This idea of truth being a major component of worship is also not new. Throughout history, Israel performed acts of worship while the worshippers themselves were living contrary to how God intended—cheating, lying, murdering, rendering injustice—as if God didn't notice their deviant lifestyles. Through His prophets, God made it very clear that He wasn't impressed with their acts or forms of worship. What He always wanted throughout the biblical narrative was worshippers who worshipped Him with "clean hands and a pure heart" (Ps. 24:4); a people who would call on Him in song while they "let justice roll down like waters" (Amos 5:24); voices that blessed God and did not curse one another because "these things ought not be so" (James 3:10). God has always spoken against the duality of worship and behavior from those who call themselves His worshippers, "people [who] draw near with their mouth / and honor me with their lips, / while their hearts are far from me" (Isa. 29:13). Jesus makes it clear in John 4:24 that truth, as a context and component of our worship, is important to the Father.

Jesus also mentions the word *spirit*. We can't see or touch a spirit yet He makes clear that this unseen element must be present in worship in order for God to pay attention. How do we quantify something unquantifiable? It is difficult to recognize something we cannot visibly see. How do we make sure we have planned for enough spirit to be present in our worship experience for it to be meaningful and even acceptable to the object of our worship? There is a mysterious element here that defies human logic and tactile experience. According to Jesus, *spirit* is central to what the Father is looking for in the worshippers He is seeking. So what is spirit?

The apostle Paul tells us that things that are seen are temporal, things that are unseen are eternal (see 2 Cor. 4:18). Is the *unseen* present in our corporate worship gatherings? Do we believe that we are worshipping the Spirit-God because we cannot see Him? Israel couldn't see Him either yet the element of *spirit* seemed to be missing in much of their worship practice as well. Are we simply talking about blind faith or is there more to it? If His unseen presence is detectable, what does it feel like? What happens when this invisible Spirit-God is worshipped in spirit and truth? Is it enough to walk away from a building each week and assume, "Well, we worshipped God by what we did this morning"? Or is there a tangible way to know that His presence was detected or manifested in our human experience? Contrarily, is there a way to know that His unseen presence was nowhere to be found?

Christians know that experiencing God transforms lives. Sometimes that change is instant; but for most of us, the changes of godliness happen over a lifetime. But what of our weekly worship? Is what we are getting out of our worship services really worship in the same way Jesus talks about to the woman in John 4? How do we know we are worshipping Him in spirit and in truth, as He has so clearly stated to be His Father's desire?

By now, you may be frustrated because I have asked many questions and provided few answers. Perhaps asking the questions is enough. The Rabbi who sat at the well also said, "Ask, and it will be given to you; seek, and you will find; knock, and it will be opened to you. For everyone who asks receives, and the one who seeks finds, and to the one who knocks it will be opened" (Matt. 7:7–8). When was the last time you spent time asking these kinds of questions about the Father's heart on worship? Why not this weekend, after services on Sunday, or tonight?

Worship founded on external factors such as location, culture, style, and even ethnic background—which, in the case of the John 4 conversation, pitted Samaritans against Jews—becomes worship that is not centered on God, the object of worship. When our worship is centered on anything other than the object of worship, it can become nothing more than wallpaper worship. Maybe Jesus was telling the Samaritan woman that her ways of worship and the Jews' ways of worship were both simply wallpaper worship. He made it clear in that conversation that worship is about engaging the heart of God, not contingent on forms or external trappings but through truth, honesty, and humility. She demonstrated the smallest level of truth and nonpretense when she admitted, "I have no husband." Perhaps that is why Jesus used Samaritans as an example of not only how to be but also what to do. This must have infuriated many of His followers. Does it make you feel the same way when you consider that what we call worship may actually be just wallpaper worship?

PART ONE:

WHAT WORSHIP IS

3

WORSHIP IS OUR HERITAGE

All that now is will be forgotten in the days to come.

Ecclesiastes 2:16, NKJV

Wallpaper worship has been around since the garden of Eden. Its first possible appearance was when God came looking for His hiding humans and asked, "Adam, where are you?" Since then, God's people have hidden behind rituals, traditions, rules, denominations, and dogmas. For instance, some worshippers are uncomfortable when wine is served in Communion alongside grape juice. Others argue about sprinkling water instead of immersion (and vice versa) during baptisms. When a suggestion is made to consider celebrating Lent for forty days in preparation for Easter, an evangelical may scold, "We don't do that. That's a Catholic thing." If someone suggests a Bible study to a Catholic, they may say, "We don't do that. The priest does that for us." When a piece of historical liturgy is introduced into a contemporary service, the musicians on the platform may stare up at the ceiling in boredom. When someone demonstratively expresses joy in a liturgical setting, they may be looked upon with disdain and judged as a "wild charismatic."

Wallpaper worship, in a rollicking contemporary setting or a dead liturgical one, has no link to its authentic or historic origins. A gathering of worshippers performing movements and sounds that look and seem like worship is wallpaper worship. It has little to do with style, culture, or setting. Wherever it happens, its participants can leave the gathering never having experienced the presence of the God they came to worship. We can also become so accustomed to wallpaper worship that we can hide from God's presence while engaging in our rituals, thinking "I'm just doing my 'worship thing' and it will make me feel better."

Biblical and church history is rife with periods when believers gathered to worship, but the worship they practiced had little resemblance to the intent behind it. In those situations, the worshippers may have "done their thing" but may not have experienced God's presence in ways they were hoping. Let's first look at a few examples in the Bible, and then we'll briefly look at a few examples from church history.

A MAN NAMED MOSES

Starting in Exodus chapter 3 with Moses' encounter with the burning bush, God orchestrates the release of His people from Egypt's bondage by informing Moses: "When you have brought the people out of Egypt, you shall worship God at this mountain" (3:12, NASB). After five chapters of plagues, sent by God to demonstrate His power to Israel's captors (chapters

7–11), Israel makes its grand exodus from Egypt (chapter 12). After the parting of the Red Sea and the drowning of Pharaoh's army (chapter 14), the Israelites finally arrive at the mountain to worship God. When they get there, Moses climbs to the top to receive God's instructions (chapter 19) and, when he returns to tell the people what God said—which is essentially a recitation of the Ten Commandments—the people notice God's presence in the form of thunder, lightning, and a huge cloud of smoke. They said to Moses, "You speak to us, and we will listen; but do not let God speak to us, lest we die" (Exod. 20:19). After that, he returned to the mountaintop to receive more of God's instructions.

During Moses' extended absence on the mountain (chapters 20–31), the Israelites demanded that their leaders help them fashion a god of their own to worship (32:1). The idea of interacting directly with God in a posture of worship can be intimidating when we are busy fashioning a god of our own preference to worship and, as a result, God's presence was nowhere near His worshippers—because they chose to worship a god of their own design. Later, in Exodus 33:3, God tells Moses, "Go up to a land flowing with milk and honey; but I will not go up among you . . . for you are a stiff-necked people." Moses entreats God throughout this passage (see 33:12–13), reminding Him of His promise to Israel and the favor he found in God's sight. In verse 14, God changed His mind and said, "My presence will go with you." Moses' response: "If your presence will not go with me, do not bring us up from here" (33:15). How many times have we "gone up" into God's presence in a worship setting and left feeling "where was God in all that?" That feeling of performing worship without the presence of God is wallpaper worship. Moses would not have any of it. Neither should we.

Similarly, in Isaiah 29:13 and Amos 5:21–23, God makes it clear that He is not impressed with the words, rituals, songs, and music presented by those gathered to worship Him. In fact, in Amos 5:23 God commands the worshippers to "take away from me the noise of your songs." So is it a stretch to imagine a group of people gathered, singing their songs, performing their rituals of worship, to a God who isn't listening or even present? I don't think it's a stretch. I think it's wallpaper worship.

A PRIEST NAMED ZECHARIAH

In the first chapter of the Gospel according to Luke, an elderly descendant of Aaron named Zechariah encounters an angel of the Lord while he is executing his priestly ritual in the Temple. The angel tells Zechariah that his barren wife, Elizabeth, is going to bear him a son. As Zechariah questions the news, the angel strikes him mute until the baby is born to prove the message is from God. The story goes on to describe a visit between Zechariah's pregnant wife, Elizabeth, and her young cousin Mary, who is already pregnant with Jesus, and how Elizabeth's baby leaps in her womb upon hearing Mary's greeting. After the birth of his son, Zechariah gets his voice back and names his son John, as he was instructed to do by the angel.

This angelic announcement, the muting of Zechariah, and eventually Mary's visit all began while Zechariah is performing a worship ritual to his God who is not present to receive it. Why? The temple rituals were faithfully performed year after year, even though the manifest presence of God had not been in the Temple for four hundred years. Even the fact that Zechariah is the priest who performs the temple ritual that day is by chance because he drew the lot cast by his fellow priests (see Luke 1:9). He walks into the Temple alone and proceeds to the Holy Place to ceremonially light the holy incense in worship. In verse 10, Luke records that a multitude of people waited outside, praying as Zechariah entered the Holy Place. What did the multitude of people outside the Temple expect to happen? Why were they in prayer? Whatever the reason, they must have known, as did Zechariah, that God's presence had not shown up in the Temple for generations. Yet these acts of worship and prayer were practiced in obedience year after year, generation after generation, albeit to a God who never showed up.[1]

In the Broadway musical *Chicago*, there is a lawyer who is very adept at deceiving gullible juries to achieve acquittal for his obviously guilty clients. In a scene too close to reality, he tap dances and sings in front of a jury.

Give 'em the old razzle dazzle
Razzle Dazzle 'em
Give 'em an act with lots of flash in it
And the reaction will be passionate
Give 'em the old hocus-pocus
Bead and feather 'em . . .
When you're in trouble, go into your dance.[2]

Perhaps the priests and spectators of Israel were accustomed to giving Yahweh the "old razzle dazzle" ritual in an empty temple. To their credit, they did this in obedience to

God's commands. Yet after four hundred years of not experiencing His presence in temple worship, perhaps they had come to expect very little in their worship experience. Since there had been no word from God through any prophets for four hundred years, the Temple dilapidated, the Holy of Holies violated,[3] their exercise of worship must have felt like a routine of sheer obedience with little or no results, akin to a one-way conversation.

WALLPAPER WORSHIP IN CHURCH HISTORY

This one-way conversation not only happened throughout biblical history, but also in periods of church history as well. Imagine hordes of peasants throughout medieval Europe strolling into huge cathedrals to go through the motions of the Roman Catholic Mass. Many could not read or write. Neither could they understand what was being recited because the Mass was performed in Latin, which was not their native tongue. Since Latin was primarily the language of the educated, noble, rich, and privileged—ahem, the church leadership—the commoners simply filled seats while the Mass was performed for them. Perhaps they were told, "This is worship. If you don't show up, you are not worshipping." For hundreds of years their parents and grandparents attended. This was all they knew. So they went week after week, generation after generation. Perhaps they went expecting nothing because for so long, they worshipped images and icons representing a God whose manifest presence seemed virtually absent. Worship was done to them and for them. What we call the Dark Ages (AD 300–AD 1520) lasted much longer than four hundred years of Israel's experience of no word from God, no manifest presence in the Temple.

THE REFORMATION

As the church grew throughout the Middle Ages, so did its political influence. With the enmeshment of church hierarchy and government monarchies, authentic worship of God took second place to pressing matters of rules, papal authorities, finances, and man-made centralized power. Martin Luther's "Ninety-five Theses," which challenged the biblical and theological validity of many of the practices of the church, became the instrument behind the Reformation of the early sixteenth century. Luther's challenge of the church's practice of selling to its parishioners "indulgences" for the mercy and forgiveness of God (for sins, past, present, and future), was heard all over Europe. Those who joined in the protest became known as Protestants. The implications of the Reformation on worship, both personal and corporate, were far reaching and remain to this day. ("Ein feste Burg ist unser Gott" or "A Mighty Fortress Is Our God," written by Martin Luther, became known as the hymn of the Reformation and is still in use.) Luther's teachings promoted the idea of "the priesthood of the believer" (see 1 Pet. 2:9). The Reformation's influence affected how Christians saw themselves as worshippers of God. Believers were able to read the Bible for themselves in their native language, pray to God, and express themselves in worship, without the mediation, interpretation, or mouthpiece of a priest or leaders designated by papal authority and rule.

It is important to understand that prior to the Reformation, worshippers were used to worship being performed *for* them, on a platform in the front of the church. They were told when to stand, when to kneel, when to sit, what to speak, and how to melodically chant. Generally the only point in the Mass in which the common worshipper was allowed to personally participate was the Eucharist (Communion). When people attend church for generations, passively watching others on a platform perform acts of worship on their behalf, and then someone like Luther comes along and declares them free to express themselves in worship—and the people can't run fast enough and far enough away from the old way of worship—it should tell us something. Did worshippers run from the presence of the God they desired to worship? Or did they run from leaders who stood in the way of sincere worship?

THE MOVEMENTS

Throughout this book, I will refer to a movement in the late 1960s and 1970s that became known as the Jesus movement. I will mention John and Charles Wesley's Methodist movement (the Great Awakening), and also a more recent movement among Christian men called Promise Keepers, which I was personally involved in at the leadership level. I will also talk about the Catholic Council known as Vatican II. Although not a movement necessarily, Vatican II had the same effect as a movement in that it affected, in significant ways, how worshippers viewed themselves and how the church worships. The point to understand here is that throughout church history, God has caused movements among His people, from outside of the mainstream church, that eventually caused significant changes to the status quo of the mainstream church. Many of these movements started because worshippers felt there must be more to the spiritual experience of worship than what the church was leading them in at the time. The Reformation (sixteenth century), the Great Awakenings (eighteenth & nineteenth centuries), the D.L. Moody Crusades (late nineteenth century), the Azusa Street Revivals (early twentieth century), the Billy Graham Crusades (twentieth century), the Jesus movement, and Promise Keepers (late twentieth century)—and there are others—all took place outside of, and in spite of, the organized church, not because of it.

History provides context in the same way a mirror provides reflection. King Solomon said, "All that now is will be forgotten in the days to come" (Eccles. 2:16, NKJV). To not know or understand our heritage as worshippers of Christ and who gave us that heritage, as well as to fail to develop a perspective based on our worship heritage is the equivalent of what the apostle James refers to as someone who observes his face in a mirror but walks away forgetting what he looked like (see James 1:24). Digging deeper into church worship history in all its details and implications is beyond the scope of this book. For now, let's just stick a shovel in the soil, and upturn the blade a little. We may discover some startling parallels to how we, as worshippers, have come full circle. My desire here is not to reconnect us to old, tired, dead rituals or bland history; but, rather, for us to understand the larger meaning of why we do what we do when we gather to worship. If worship is expressing "devotion to a deity" as *Webster's American English Dictionary* defines it, and we as Christians claim that Deity (God the Father, Son, and Spirit) has changed our lives, then perhaps it is crucial for us to recognize whose shoulders we stand on when we do this thing called worship.

WORSHIP IS OUR HERITAGE

I am amazed at how many believers think *worship* started with Integrity or Hillsong Publishing. Perhaps it is easy to jump to that conclusion when we spot these or other publisher names on large screens projecting song lyrics. Or for a new believer who has never been exposed to church music, liturgy, or worship styles prior to the year 2000, it is quite easy to think this worship phenomenon is new. I hate to disappoint you, but even the good people at the Christian music publishing companies will assure you: Worship didn't start with them! So fly with me now at thirty thousand feet elevation. Let's get the perspective that comes from seeing this heritage of worship in context. As we do, we will see the sheer intentionality of God to bring us into His worship covey. Being a worshipper of God is not something that happens by chance. This is a gift, designed and delivered by God Himself. It's up to us to unwrap it.

Have you ever participated in a Secret Santa game? Whenever I find out we are going to a party around Christmastime and the Secret Santa game will be played, I kind of inwardly groan. But after my wife, Angela, takes us shopping for a few gifts to take, it actually turns out to be fun as well as revealing. Here's how it goes: Unbeknownst to you, your name is given to someone who is going to leave you gifts over a period of weeks or days prior to Christmas. In the beginning, everyone is excited about receiving their gifts. But the game becomes more meaningful when you find out who your Secret Santa is. The gifts take on a richer meaning when that person's identity is revealed and they share the reasons why they chose each gift specifically for you. In the end, you discover that, as much fun as it is to receive gifts, the game is actually about your Secret Santa's thoughtfulness and intentionality.

Understanding our heritage as worshippers is understanding God's thoughtfulness and intentionality. John 1:12 states, "as many as received Him, to them He gave the right to become children of God" (NASB) Is it amiss to say the same of becoming worshippers of God? I don't think so. Let's look at this gift of worship we have inherited.

WHO GAVE CHRISTIAN BELIEVERS THIS HERITAGE OF WORSHIPPING GOD?

The answer is *the Jews*. The earliest records we have of the worship of the Hebrew God is the Old Testament. The book of Genesis teaches it was through Abraham that the "promise of God" would be passed down, first to his own people and ultimately to all people.

> When Abram was ninety-nine years old the LORD appeared to Abram and said to him, "I am God Almighty; walk before me, and be blameless, that I may make my covenant between me and you, and may multiply you greatly." Then Abram fell on his face. And God said to him, "Behold, my covenant is with you, and you shall be the father of a multitude of nations. . . . I will make you exceedingly fruitful, and I will make you into nations, and kings shall come from you. And I will establish my covenant between me and you and your offspring after you throughout their generations for an everlasting

covenant, to be God to you and to your offspring
after you. (Gen. 17:1–7)

Later, in the Gospel of Matthew 1:1–17, the birth line of
Jesus Christ is traced directly forward starting with Abraham.
This is important to know: Jesus was a Jew. And since Jesus
is the object of Christian worship through the ages, Gentile
believers should understand that the very acts of worship we
practice are fruits of a tree planted in Israel. Our worship of
Jesus the Christ—the Jewish Messiah—is fulfillment of God's
covenant with Abraham. We are among those descendants
He mentions in Genesis 17.

Matthew 1:2–16 outlines Jesus' lineage starting with Abraham
and ending with Jesus' earthly father, Joseph. Verse 17 makes a
final wrap-up statement: "All the generations from Abraham
to David were fourteen generations, and from David to
the deportation to Babylon fourteen generations, and from
the deportation to Babylon to the Christ [Jesus] fourteen
generations."

So Jesus' practices of prayer, observation of the Sabbath,
hearing the law and prophets read aloud, worship in the synagogue, and yearly temple sacrifice, which He observed His
family practicing from early boyhood, were passed down
to Him through His Hebrew heritage. Later in the New
Testament, in the letter to the Romans, Paul makes a bold
statement about this to the Gentiles at the church in Rome.
He tells them not to forget their roots as having come from
Israel and her history as the chosen ones of God, as the first
worshippers of God. "Remember it is not you who support
the root, but the root that supports you" (Rom. 11:18).

It seems fundamental to understand the origin of our God-worship was from the Hebrew people. Upon visiting a church in Texas, my mother (who was a teacher on the Hebrew roots of the Christian faith) noticed printed Sunday school materials in the children's department. There was a picture of Jesus with blonde hair and blue eyes, complete with a caption line: "Jesus was a good Christian boy who went to Sunday school each Sunday." After two thousand years of history, education, industry, technology, and church planting, many people who attend church still have no idea who laid the foundation for their weekly worship of almighty God.

THE TORN VEIL

So the Jews were the first to worship this God who identified Himself throughout history as the one true Creator. But at what point was the practice of God-worship passed to non-Jews? This worship inheritance began for Gentiles at a very specific moment inside the temple in Jerusalem, after Jesus' death outside the city. There were many significant moments as Jesus was being crucified, but two verses from Matthew's Gospel provide the hinge point for this gift of worship being given to non-Jews: "Jesus cried out again with a loud voice and yielded up his spirit. And behold, the curtain of the temple was torn in two, from top to bottom" (27:50–51).

According to biblical scholars, the veil (curtain) of the Temple was a thick, interwoven curtain that guarded the entrance of what was known as the Holy of Holies. This was where God's manifest presence dwelt for many generations long past. Once a year, the priest would enter past the curtain into the very presence of God to offer a blood sacrifice of atonement in exchange for God's forgiveness of the sins of the people. The Holy of Holies was located inside the Temple and was accessed through what was called the inner chamber. So the curtain dividing the Holy of Holies from the inner chamber hung from girders that were attached to load-bearing supports inside the temple structure. We will see later why the interior structure is important.

Solomon's temple, referred to as the first temple and built nine hundred years before Christ, was sixty cubits in height, meaning the curtain was hung approximately ninety feet high. The second temple during Jesus' time, which was built on a constructed square the length of six football fields, rose to a height of approximately twenty stories. Since the curtain was hung from the inside, it could have been at a height of approximately ten stories (100–150 feet) and 4–6 inches in thickness.

DIAGRAM OF THE TEMPLE

HOLY OF HOLIES   HOLY PLACE   VESTIBULE

Since the Temple was where priests would offer to God the blood of animals to atone for the sins of the people, this ripping of the veil was highly significant. The tearing of the veil from top to bottom in the temple in Jerusalem that day was later interpreted as a sign that the death of Jesus was the final blood sacrifice for sins for all time: "He did not enter by means of the blood of goats and calves; but he entered the Most Holy Place once for all by his own blood, thus obtaining eternal redemption" (Heb. 9:12, NIV).

Suddenly, the most intimate acts of worship were no longer hidden behind a man-made barrier. The words of the old Jewish prophets leapt from the ancient manuscripts to verify the meaning of Jesus' death and the interpretation of the torn veil in the Temple,

> Behold, the days are coming, declares the LORD, when I will make a new covenant with the house of Israel and the house of Judah. . . . For this is the covenant that I will make with the house of Israel after those days, declares the LORD: I will put my law within them, and I will write it on their hearts. And I will be their God, and they shall be my people. And no longer shall each one teach his neighbor and each his brother, saying, 'Know the LORD,' for they shall all know me, from the least of them to the greatest, declares the LORD. For I will forgive their iniquity, and I will remember their sin no more. (Jer. 31:31–34)

The significance of the torn veil was that this holy place, previously forbidden to see or enter, was now visible and approachable by anyone, even the very least, not simply the elite high priests, who were the greatest. Could this have been a dramatic illustration that something new had begun for non-Jews?

How the curtain was torn was also a phenomenon packed with symbolism. The rip itself started from the top and traveled to the bottom, signifying God's finger was the one that accomplished it. Had it been from bottom to top there would still be arguments suggesting human intervention. But if that were so, how does someone rip a curtain made of woven fabric that is 4–6 inches thick and 150 feet high? How would the perpetrators get into the inner chamber to pull it off? The fact that the curtain was surrounded by structure, hanging from interior supports attached to load-bearing girders is a curious sign. If the curtain was hanging inside, but the Temple had no roof, it could be said the curtain was weakened by exposure to outside elements, such as the change in weather that occurred during the crucifixion.

To this day, the torn veil has made a massive statement to the world. That which was closed—His holy, sinless dwelling place—is now opened. It is as if God Himself threw open the front door to the throne room of His palace to announce to all nations, all races, all peoples throughout history:

Come see what I have done.

Let all come before me as the priests once did.

But bring no blood sacrifice.

Because of My son's sacrifice, now you are all priests.

My door is open for all people, for all time.

Jew, come and worship Me.

Gentile, come and worship Me.

Like Christmas wrapping paper being torn, the veil represents God Himself unwrapping His gift to Gentiles of every race and nation, honoring His ageless covenant to Abraham. What once belonged exclusively to the Jews now belongs to anyone who comes to God by faith. "Understand, then, that those who have faith are children of Abraham. Scripture foresaw that God would justify the Gentiles by faith, and announced the gospel in advance to Abraham: 'All nations will be blessed through you.' So those who rely on faith are blessed along with Abraham, the man of faith" (Gal. 3:7–9, NIV)

As Gentiles, we now have membership into something so large, so deep, so wide. Could it be that a deep awareness of our heritage is that which attracts the presence of God Himself, the originator of that heritage and the very object of our worship? With such a deep heritage, why do we settle for wallpaper worship? A.W. Tozer points out, "Because worship is largely missing, do you know what we are doing? We are doing our best to sew up that rent veil in the temple. . . . We use artificial means to try to induce some kind of worship."[4]

PROMISE KEEPERS

From 1991–1997, a spiritual awakening swept the United States. The "men's movement," as it became known, took place in huge events known as Promise Keepers (PK). Men from every denomination, race, and geographic location gathered in NFL-sized stadiums to renew their commitment to fulfilling promises they made to God, their wives, their children, and their communities. These events, attended exclusively by men, were the largest of their kind in United States history.

The PK events were started in Boulder, Colorado by the University of Colorado's head football coach, Bill McCartney, who led the team to a national championship title in 1990. Following that successful season, he used his platform to call Christian men together to renew and keep their promises. In 1992, Folsom Stadium at the University of Colorado was half full, with about twenty-five thousand in attendance. A year later, it was sold out. In 1994, six PK events were held in locations around the country. The next year, they more than doubled. By 1996, PK held events in twenty-six NFL and college football stadiums, all packed with men singing, praying, and listening to nationally known authors and pastors and contemporized worship music. For three days, PK sponsored a clergy conference at the Georgia Dome in Atlanta, the largest gathering of clergy in history. The movement culminated in October 1997 in Washington, DC, where more than a million men gathered on the National Mall for a day of prayer, fasting, and worship.

It was a movement unlike any other seen in our lifetime. It was as if the men of God across all lines within Christianity came together to say, "We have been passive, we have not led, we have not loved. We repent, and we will keep our promises." On the opening nights of many events, it was not uncommon to see six thousand men walk down to the stage on the field to make a personal commitment to follow Christ. It was truly an exciting time.

I was hired in 1995 to head the program and production team for those events. My wife, Angela, had just given birth to our third child; and we were preparing to move from Franklin, Tennessee, where we'd lived for five years to be closer to the burgeoning Christian music business. With our newborn daughter, Alisha, in tow and our other two children—our five-year-old son, Jeremy, and four-year-old daughter, Corina —we moved from Tennessee back to Colorado to join the staff of this exploding organization. My job was to oversee the music, speakers, and messages and manage each event as the on-site director and producer, calling cues and making program changes as necessary.

In summer 1996, we were almost sold out at Legion Field at the University of Alabama at Birmingham. I remember it well because it rained the entire weekend and the stadium had no roof. More than fifty thousand men sat there in rain gear and under trash bags Friday night and all day Saturday. We were constantly checking the weather to see if we would get a break in the storm. It didn't look likely. But I will never forget what happened on Saturday morning.

PK was partnering with local messianic churches and, as program director, I was tasked with finding a messianic rabbi who would open the Saturday morning portion of the program by saying the Shema, the Jewish prayer found in Deuteronomy 6 ("Hear, O Israel!"), in Hebrew. That recitation would be followed by the blowing of the ram's horn called the shofar. It was our way of remembering our heritage as worshippers, a way of giving tribute to the Jewish roots of our Christian faith.

That rainy Saturday we arrived at the stadium hoping for some good news about the weather, but that good news never came. The emcee introduced the rabbi, a young man in his thirties, and his cantor, who blew the shofar after the rabbi prayed. When those two men took the stage in traditional Jewish clothing, the rain stopped. When the rabbi gave the Shema in Hebrew, he didn't just read it—he yelled it. At that exact moment, the clouds parted, the sun shined into the stadium, and fifty thousand men jumped to their feet shouting in praise to God. The moment the rabbi left the stage, the clouds moved together to hide the sun and the rain started again.

When the rabbi came off the stage and visited my tent at stage right, I said to him, "Did you see that? Did you see what just happened?"

"Yes, of course," he said nonchalantly. "God likes to hear His language."

A HERITAGE OF RETELLING AND REENACTMENT

God not only likes hearing His language, He also enjoys showing His power when His own story is being retold and reenacted. The Hebrew people were excellent at passing down their heritage. Much of that was done through oral tradition and scribes. The fact that generations of Jews could retell the stories of Noah, Abraham, Isaac, Jacob, Joseph, and Moses with such accuracy shows how important passing down their heritage of worship was to them as a people. In his classic book *Worship Is a Verb*, Robert Webber talks about the drama of worship. It is a retelling and reenactment of a series of stories regarding what God has done for us. These stories of our faith heritage are told "with words attended by power—the power to recreate the event, to draw people into the event, and to result in their repentance, conversion, and commitment."[5]

If we are committed to passing down our heritage, we must be committed to retelling the stories of God's greatness, not simply our responses to His greatness. If the stories and songs we hear in weekly worship exclusively retell what God did last week in someone's life, it can be like skipping the main course and dining only on dessert. These personal stories, sweet as they can be, are not always based on His power, His acts, or His greatness that have been relayed through the ancient Scriptures for generations before us and will be told for generations to follow. They are told through a grid of present personal experience, which may have little connection with what we have inherited and what has stood the test of time.

Not only is there a retelling, but also reenactment. Each year, the Jews reenact the Passover meal in their homes, synagogues, and community centers. The miracle of God setting His people free from the bondage of Egyptian slavery is renewed in the hearts and minds of worshippers. Webber continues, "The purpose of the Passover seder (Haggadah) is to not only recite past events, but to bring them into the present."[6] The heritage is passed down. Christians likewise are called to reenact the Passover, retold through Jesus, the Passover Lamb Himself. The heritage of being delivered from the bondage of sin is passed down. This retelling and reenactment are disciplines in worship and have yielded some of the greatest music, drama, and art the world has seen.

SPENDING OUR INHERITANCE

Anyone who has reached a recognition of their life's trajectory in sin—who has made a decision to reverse that trajectory and receive God's gift of adoption and eternal life through His Son's sacrifice on the cross—is on their way to enjoying their inheritance. That is who the Christian is. That is the God-worshipper. A person like that doesn't struggle with how to worship any more than a baby struggles with how to breathe. A person touched by and changed by God has plenty of prayers and songs through which to say "thank you" to Him. There is nothing as exuberant as a new Christian expressing gratitude for all they have received through their newfound faith. There is nothing as inspiring as an old Christian who loves to serve and worship, bringing the maturity and gratitude of experience to the community of believers.

Jesus said the Father is seeking worshippers who will worship Him in spirit and in truth (see John 4:23). Recognizing who passed this gift on to us as Gentiles creates a deep sense of privilege, an inner awareness that we are an extension of history. With each act of worship in which we participate, we are writing our own story in the history of this ancient practice of worshipping the true Creator. What a privilege that God chose to include the non-Jew.

When it comes to how we worship, Jews and Christians differ a lot. When it comes to the God we worship, Christians share much with the Jews. The same Moses whom the Jews have followed for generations appeared on the Mount of Transfiguration visiting with Jesus, whom Gentiles follow (see Matt. 17:1–3). The Passover celebrated each year by Jews is the same Passover on which Jesus was crucified as the "Lamb of God, who takes away the sin of the world" (John 1:29). Peter, the apostle, quotes the Jewish prophet Joel and King David of Israel as proof to a Jewish audience on the day of Pentecost that this Jesus was, in fact, the promised Messiah (see Acts 2). Later, Peter is told by God in a vision that the gospel is not just for the Jew, but for the Gentile as well (see Acts 10). What a privilege that God chose to include Gentiles as worshippers. As the psalmist said: "For the LORD will not forsake his people; he will not abandon his heritage" (Ps. 94:14). Indeed, God has not only not abandoned His heritage, He has passed it along to all throughout history. Shouldn't we do the same? We have such a vast, rich, and deep heritage of worship. Let's pass it on.

So how are you spending your inheritance? Is worship something you do simply because your parents or grandparents did? Are you hearing songs or recitations of Scripture in a language you barely understand? Have you gone through sacramental rituals like Communion, baptism, or confirmation without an awareness of where these sacraments began, and why they are worthy tools of worship from a grateful heart? Are we aware of the shoulders we stand on when we walk into a place of worship? Or is our worship experience one that is similar to that of Zechariah? Are we worshipping a God we feel is absent? Is our worship a vibrant, powerful, and participatory experience? Or is our worship actually wallpaper worship?

4

WORSHIP IS OUR PRIVILEGE

What a privilege to carry everything to God in prayer.
  —Joseph Scriven, "What a Friend We Have in Jesus"

Enjoying the benefits of an inheritance is a privilege, especially since, by its definition, an inheritance is never required to be paid back. It is a gift. Its beneficiaries can draw on those funds for free. How they use their inheritance is as varied as their personalities. Inheritances can change lives, which is one of the reasons why benefactors bequeath them in the first place. The opportunity to see and experience things we normally would not be able to see and experience has a way of changing our perspective. It is the perspective of privilege.

THE YEAR OF 1863

In 1863, the United States was no longer *united states*. We were divided by differences in policy on issues such as states' rights, federal control, industry versus agriculture, and most prominently, the interpretation of our founders' words: "We hold these truths to be self-evident, that all men are created equal." The future of slavery in America had not only reached a boiling point, it spilled over into a horrible Civil War. The debate had already grown so heated that in 1859, arguments broke out in the Washington, DC legislature, complete with fists, knives, and pistols.[1] By the next year, Southern states had broken away from the Union to form the Confederacy and war ensued. No one could have predicted the magnitude and agony that would consume the country.

July 1863 is remembered as the summer of the Battle of Gettysburg, one of the bloodiest battles of the entire war as well as a turning point for the Union. Later that same year, President Abraham Lincoln gave his Gettysburg Address, which would become one of the most famous speeches in history. A few years earlier, a man named Joseph Scriven composed a poem that was later set to a tune and became one of the most beloved hymns of all time.

> What a friend we have in Jesus,
> All our sins and griefs to bear!
> What a privilege to carry
> Everything to God in prayer![2]

We don't know much of the story behind his lyrics. What we do know is what was happening in Scriven's world during that time in history. The grief that Americans in the North and South were bearing because of a war that had no end in sight was overwhelming. The devastation of lives, homes, farms, and family fortunes, along with the displacement of thousands, was maddening. Yet Scriven knew something all Christians should know: No matter what happens to us or around us, we can carry "everything to God in prayer." He maintained the perspective of privilege during an extremely difficult period that has been relevant in every era. The ability to assume a prayerful posture is itself an act of worship—and what a privilege it is.

FAVORED VANTAGE POINT

Years ago, American Express ran an ad campaign that proclaimed "membership has its privileges." If you were approved for a card, you were part of a group that had certain advantages, which gave you a perspective from a favored vantage point. The ad campaign was successful because it convinced people that if they had an American Express card, they would live a privileged life. The same is true about our heritage of worshipping God. We have been given a favored vantage point that, according to the New Testament, even the angels long to have.

> Concerning this salvation, the prophets, who spoke of the grace that was to come to you, searched intently and with the greatest care, trying to find out the time and circumstances to which the Spirit of Christ in them was pointing when he predicted the sufferings of the Messiah and the glories that would follow. It was revealed to them that they were not serving themselves but you, when they spoke of the things that have now been told you by those who have preached the gospel to you by the

> Holy Spirit sent from heaven. Even angels long to
> look into these things. (1 Pet. 1:10–12, NIV)

Are the angels really envious of us? According to Peter, they long to see God's plan from the perspective we have been given. Think about this. All we have inherited in Christ's death and resurrection was revealed to the prophets who predicted the time of Christ, His sufferings, and the glories that would follow. Now, those who have received this inheritance get to enjoy it with their fellow believers Sunday after Sunday, week after week, all the days of their lives. The angels saw it all from afar. We are at the center of the action. What this passage tells us is that we have a favored vantage point. What we are a part of, given to us by those who went before us, has been revealed and announced to us first. We are in on something that is unique, with a firsthand view that is up close and personal.

ORCHESTRA LEVEL, CENTER SECTION, ROW 1, SEAT 1

It is as if God purchased for all of us front row seats to the greatest event of all time. No rear balcony or nosebleed end zone seats that require binoculars. No TV screens to passively watch secondhand. We all have been moved up to the front row—to see God's plan in person and enjoy His gift firsthand. What you and I see, experience, feel, hear, read, and sing about every week in our church worship services is done from a favored vantage point where we can view our lives, history, and redemption from a completely new and different perspective. Do we realize what this can mean for corporate worship as the church? Are you catching the vision that if every churchgoer brought a perspective of privilege into their place of worship, our corporate worship could be transformed into a rich, real experience for everyone? There would be no wallpaper worship.

A perspective of privilege is where the apostle Paul was coming from when he wrote, "Not that I am speaking of being in need, for I have learned in whatever situation I am to be content" (Phil. 4:11). The prophet Habakkuk had a perspective of privilege in the midst of his people's destruction when he wrote,

> Though the fig tree should not blossom,
>   nor fruit be on the vines,
> the produce of the olive fail
>   and the fields yield no food,
> the flock be cut off from the fold
>   and there be no herd in the stalls,
> yet I will rejoice in the LORD;
>   I will take joy in the God of my salvation.
>   (3:17–18)

A perspective of privilege is not only a powerful motivator in worship; it can transform our lives as believers.

It is no surprise that in a year of death and destruction like 1863, believers could say with conviction, "What a privilege to carry everything to God in prayer." Gaining a perspective of privilege does not usually happen in the middle of great prosperity or easy living. This kind of eternal perspective is usually gained through loss.

WHEN THE SUN IS SHINING OR NOT

In Philippians 3:10, Paul writes, "that I may know him and the power of his resurrection, and may share his sufferings, becoming like him in his death." A close look at each phrase indicates seasons of our lives in which we know and walk with God. For instance, who doesn't want to know the power of His resurrection? It is the point where triumph overcomes failure, light overtakes darkness, success overpowers defeat, life swallows death. The power of His resurrection is what makes Christianity Christian and separates it from every other religious belief in the world. No one else conquered death by reversing its course and canceling its effects. What was never reversible became just that, as the Nazarene's burial clothes laid empty and lifeless in a tomb, without a body to occupy them.

As the days unfolded after His horrific death on a Roman cross, He was physically seen and encountered in the flesh by His followers, friends, and strangers on the road to Emmaus. He appeared without announcement, behind closed doors, to His closest followers and held out His hands for them to observe and even feel the fresh nail wounds. He picked up a piece of broiled fish to eat and declared, "A ghost does not have flesh like I have." Booyah! Neither does a ghost eat and digest a fillet of fish—whether it's broiled, grilled, or fried. This power of His resurrection is the gospel gathered to one place, one moment in time, yet spread out wide through eternity to those who call on His name.

As positive as the power of His resurrection is, I learn the perspective of privilege in the fellowship of His sufferings, being conformed even unto His death. When life unravels, I am forced into a place of hardship. There I get to watch the power of His resurrection work. There is no resurrection unless there is first death.

In their song "Blessed Be Your Name," songwriters Matt and Beth Redman wrote:

> Blessed be Your name
> When I'm found in the desert place
> Though I walk through the wilderness
> Blessed be Your name. . . .
>
> Blessed be Your name
> When the sun's shining down on me
> When the world's 'all as it should be'
> Blessed be Your name.
>
> Blessed be Your name
> On the road marked with suffering
> Though there's pain in the offering
> Blessed be Your name. . . .
>
> You give and take away . . .
> Lord, blessed be Your name.[3]

The writers of the Broadway musical *The Fantasticks* also understood this principle, reflected in their classic song "Try to Remember."

> Deep in December, it's nice to remember,
> Although you know the snow will follow.

Deep in December, it's nice to remember,
Without a hurt the heart is hollow.[4]

As confusing and contradictory as it can sound, a perspective of privilege is born from suffering. Since suffering and death are mentioned alongside the power of His resurrection in Philippians 3:10, isn't it safe to say that sharing in His suffering makes us one with Christ as much as the power of His resurrection does? The apostle Peter pairs these two realities of resurrection and suffering together in his first epistle.

> Beloved, do not be surprised at the fiery trial when it comes upon you to test you, as though something strange were happening to you. But rejoice insofar as you share Christ's sufferings, that you may also rejoice and be glad when his glory is revealed. If you are insulted for the name of Christ, you are blessed, because the Spirit of glory and of God rests upon you. (1 Pet. 4:12–14)

This is a tough reality when we spend our days working to create a life of rest and ease. No matter how hard we work toward that end, the words of Jesus override our efforts and create a different context for living life on this side of eternity. In his book *Sacred Marriage*, Gary Thomas said, "The desire for ease, comfort, and stress-free living is an indirect desire to remain an 'unseasoned,' immature Christian."[5] He is speaking in the context of the struggles in marriage. Could the same be applied in the context of worship as well? Without a perspective of privilege, the inevitable tribulation Jesus promises will bring us down, make us cynical, render us "unseasoned, immature" worshippers. John Wimber, one of the founders of the Vineyard Church movement said, "Worship is not about . . . comfort. It's about God."[6]

A THOUSAND THROATS

Martin Luther said in one of his sermons: "If you say, 'Hey, birdie, why are you so gay? You have no cook, no cellar,' he will answer, 'I do not sow, I do not reap, I do not gather into barns. But I have a cook, and his name is Heavenly Father.'"[7] Luther's sermon takes its cue from the words of Jesus in the Sermon on the Mount: "Look at the birds of the air: they neither sow nor reap nor gather into barns, and yet your heavenly Father feeds them. Are you not of more value than they?" (Matt. 6:26).

Jesus is challenging His listeners and readers to gain a heavenly perspective, which He says the birds already have. Taking this perspective into worship is something that can transform our worship into what is intended to be a weekly, daily, momentary encounter of complete and utter gratitude for being counted among the privileged.

Luther finishes his sermon thought by saying: "Fool, shame on you. You do not sing. You work all day and cannot sleep for worry. I sing as if I had a thousand throats."[8] It may have been this Lutheran reference that inspired Charles Wesley's hymn lyric: "O for a thousand tongues to sing my great Redeemer's praise!"

Perhaps people who attend church but do not sing are silent because they have no perspective of privilege. Perhaps they have no perspective of privilege because they do not recognize what God has done and is doing for us. Perhaps they don't recognize what God has done because they do not understand God's divine revelation in His Word. Perhaps they do not understand God's Word because they are not hearing it purely proclaimed. Perhaps they do not have the Spirit of God within them to remind them of all Jesus has said. If we do not have His Spirit working within us, it is either because we are by choice estranged from our heavenly Father or, worse, because we are not one of His sheep hearing His voice and following Him: "But you do not believe because you are not among my sheep. My sheep hear my voice, and I know them, and they follow me" (John 10:26–27).

Paul also makes it clear that those who are God's children can clearly hear His voice: "Now we have received not the spirit of the world, but the Spirit who is from God, that we might understand the things freely given us by God. . . . The natural person does not accept the things of the Spirit of God, for they are folly to him, and he is not able to understand them because they are spiritually discerned" (1 Cor. 2:12, 14).

The problem of corporate passivity is caused by many factors, which we will explore in more detail. But could it also be that our congregation refuses to ring out with corporate singing and praise because the attendees have little perspective of privilege? This is akin to belonging to an enormously wealthy family of power and prestige but choosing to live in the slums of a third world country, cut off from all contact with reality. When you understand the inheritance, the choice for not spending it makes no sense.

Luther was right. It is foolish to live life in such a way. It is especially uncomfortable to be standing in a church in a mute state, wondering what all the hullabaloo is about when you're surrounded by "a thousand throats," all singing and praising their God for His immeasurable goodness to them. It also seems foolish for leaders on the platform to be experiencing their own personal flush of spiritual feelings while few of their sheep are following them into the moment. Leaving the sheep behind to fend for themselves is not leading. Jesus equates it to abandonment: "He who is a hired hand and not a shepherd . . . sees the wolf coming and leaves the sheep and flees, and the wolf snatches them and scatters them. He flees because he is a hired hand and cares nothing for the sheep" (John 10:12–13).

THE WESLEYS' NEW PERSPECTIVE

When John and Charles Wesley began to work in ministry, they enthusiastically became missionaries to the American colonies. They led hundreds to Christ through their songs and preaching but it was not until the two reached a point of emptiness that they sought God's presence for themselves. What they knew of salvation was only through the works they were doing. The story of the conversion of these two brothers in ministry is a story of a complete change of perspective.

"In 1735 the brothers Wesley sailed. . . to Georgia, but even in this missionary service, the old doubts about their experience of salvation surfaced. Neither John nor Charles could find assurance that he was indeed the child of God by grace. They returned to England believing their lives and ministry had failed. John Wesley wrote. . ., 'I went to America to convert the Indians; but, oh, who shall convert me?'"

Imagine, two brothers, traveling across the Atlantic Ocean in an eighteenth-century ship to preach, sing, and lead worship services, who had not experienced for themselves what they were leading others to experience. John's question ("But Oh, who shall convert me?") rings with the confusion that probably comes to many who sit through worship services or perhaps even stand on the worship platform, who for whatever reasons do not allow themselves to be led personally into a life-changing encounter with Jesus Christ. In the Wesley's lives, their frustration of failure in ministry was from a lack of a perspective of privilege—the privilege of being a true child of God, which comes only through a personal encounter with and surrender to Jesus Christ Himself (see John 14:6).

"The answer to [John Wesley's] question came shortly after his return from America. Both he and Charles were influenced by Moravian friends who bore witness to salvation by grace through faith in Christ. Charles Wesley was the first of the two . . . to be justified by faith . . . He wrote in his journal that the Spirit of God 'chased away the darkness of my unbelief.'. . . [Charles] wrote a hymn to commemorate his day of salvation ["And Can It Be That I Should Gain"] . . . The last verse triumphantly proclaims:

> No condemnation now I dread,
> Jesus, and all in Him, is mine;
> Alive in Him, my living Head,
> And clothed in righteousness Divine,
> Bold I approach th' eternal throne,
> And claim the crown, through Christ, my own."

This Wesleyan hymn ("And Can It Be That I Should Gain") has seen a revival of its lyrics in the song "You Are My King".

Lyrics like this are timeless, as are many of the Wesleyan era hymns. Charles Wesley wrote over six thousand. This is why many of the Wesleyan hymns are used extensively in the repertoire of worship music today.

"Three days later, on May 24, 1738, John's seeking for the grace of God ended in a meeting house on Aldersgate Street in London. 'John' declared, 'I believe!' Until their conversions the Wesleys had what John described as 'a fair summer religion.' They were both ordained, preached, composed hymns, and gave themselves to missionary work—all to no avail. They had not Christ, or rather, Christ did not have them."

John immediately shared the good news with Charles. Charles wrote that "Towards ten, my brother was brought in triumph by a troop of our friends, and declared, 'I believe.' We sang the hymn with great joy, and parted with prayer."

They were both ordained. They both preached, taught, wrote, composed hymns, and even gave themselves to missionary work—all to no avail. They had not Christ, or rather, Christ did not have them.[9]

Isn't that amazing? The founders of the Methodist tradition preached, taught, wrote, composed, and performed acts for God without a true faith in God. Could this happen again? Could this be happening now? A personal encounter with God will completely change a person's perspective. It was from this new perspective of faith that the Wesleys realized how privileged they were to be called sons of God, sheep of the Shepherd, followers of Christ, leaders of worshippers. Only from a new, God-given perspective could Charles write a lyric like this: "O for a thousand tongues to sing my great Redeemer's praise, the glories of my God and King, the triumphs of his grace."[10]

In Anne Ortlund's *Up With Worship*, she describes a child watching a parade through a knothole in a fence. He sees a clown, then he sees a lion. If he sees a space in between he thinks the parade is over, or there is no parade at all. Only until he is on the shoulders of an adult, looking up over the fence, can he see the whole parade. "Now we see through a knothole . . . and we get thoroughly discouraged. True worship can change all that."[11] Our corporate worship experience could be transformed through congregants being led to a perspective of privilege, no matter what trials they may be facing.

When we understand our heritage, and the perspective of privilege it gives us, we are propelled to gratitude. Expressing our gratitude is not only an act of worship. It is our duty.

5

WORSHIP IS OUR DUTY

Piglet noticed that even though he had a very small heart,
it could hold a rather large amount of gratitude.
—A.A. Milne, *Winnie-the-Pooh*

Imagine someone invites you to dinner at their home. This is someone you barely know but you have observed they appear to be wealthy and influential. You feel a bit taken aback and nervous, but you are genuinely excited about the evening. You put together the right outfit—not too dressy or overdone, but something appropriate and up-to-date. The day arrives. You are distracted at work because of the anticipation of the evening's engagement. You wonder, *What will it be like? Will I be appropriate? I hope I don't burp.*

Finally, you arrive on time at their home. You are graciously greeted by your hosts at the door. They take your coat and invite you in like an old friend. They offer appetizers and something to sip. They have the table set to the nines: forks everywhere, china plates, crystal goblets, and a beautiful candelabra lit with long candles in the middle of a long table.

After the premeal cordials, you are led into an elaborate dining room. It is a multiple-course dinner fit for royalty. If you were to order something like this in a restaurant, you know it would cost a fortune. The wine is smooth and fine. The dessert is classy, artistic, and perfect. The conversation is all about you as they ask you questions regarding your family, your interests, and your dreams and aspirations. The evening comes to a close and it is time to go home. You feel you are part of their family, and the invitation to come by anytime for a visit is warm and sincere.

Upon your arrival home—either that evening or, at the latest, the next morning before you do anything else—what is the first thing you are supposed to do? Hint: What did your mother teach you?

Answer: Write a thank-you note.

Why: It is appropriate.

Reason: After what was done on your behalf, it is your duty.

Worship is our thank-you note to God.

MERCI, DANKE, GRAZIE, GAMSAHMNIDA

Whenever I travel internationally, the first phrase I try to learn in my host country language is "thank you." Once I get the pronunciation down and let it roll, it's amazing to see how quickly it puts a smile on the face of the hearer.

When someone holds a door open for us, bends over to pick up something we dropped, or offers to pay the tab for a meal, the natural response is to say "thank you." Actions of kindness elicit a duty of response. Lack of gratitude creates a loud disruption, birthing void where there can be relationship.

Have you ever wondered if God appreciates hearing "thank you"? In Luke 17:11–19, the story is told of Jesus and His encounter with some very sick, stinky men who were not only less than healthy, but less than grateful.

> On the way to Jerusalem he was passing along between Samaria and Galilee. And as he entered a village, he was met by ten lepers, who stood at a distance and lifted up their voices, saying, "Jesus, Master, have mercy on us." When he saw them he said to them, "Go and show yourselves to the priests." And as they went they were cleansed. Then one of them, when he saw that he was healed, turned back, praising God with a loud voice; and he fell on his face at Jesus' feet, giving him thanks. Now he was a Samaritan. Then Jesus answered, "Were not ten cleansed? Where are the nine? Was no one found to return and give praise to God except this foreigner?" And he said to him, "Rise and go your way; your faith has made you well."

Leprosy not only guaranteed a slow and horrible death; the leper was also relegated to living outside of society, even if the victim was from a wealthy or socially popular family. To be approached by ten leprous men must have been daunting to those accompanying Jesus on this journey. After these ten ugly outcasts cry out for help, Jesus gives them a challenge. He tells them to go show themselves to the priest before they are actually healed. Showing themselves to the priest was a Jewish ritual, to verify healing and cleansing and to receive acceptance back into society. Jesus' telling them to do this as they are standing there in their diseased state probably sounded ludicrous to them and those observing. The leprous men could've thought, *Is this guy nuts? We can't go to the Temple and show ourselves. We can't even get into town. We're lepers!* But choosing to obey Jesus' command was an act of faith by these men. What did they have to lose?

When only one man out of the ten returns to tell Jesus thank you, Jesus' question seems almost in surprise or dismay: "Only one returned to say thanks? Where are the others?" Do you find it interesting that Jesus asks this? Can we conclude that even God expects a thank-you note?

An interesting twist of this story is that the one man who does return to say thank you is a Samaritan, a foreigner, as Jesus calls him. Although it is not stated, the story implies the other nine were Jews, hence their familiarity with the tradition to show themselves to the priest. As we already know, Samaritans were hated by the Jews as racial outcasts. Did the others take for granted they were from a tribe known as "God's chosen?" Were they simply self-absorbed, entitled, or ungrateful?

When someone holds the door open or picks up the tab, we are conscious to make sure we express our thanks. Yet when God touches our lives, answers our prayer, rescues a son or daughter, saves a broken marriage, heals an infirmity, it is uncanny how we can forget to say thank you. It is a duty that requires humility. Or perhaps, like the Samaritan leper, it requires a physical journey back to the person or place in time through which the miracle came.

BEACH BUM GRATITUDE

Years ago, I was in Virginia Beach visiting family and friends and was able to attend their church on Sunday. It had been founded when Christians started canvasing the beach to share the good news about Jesus with whomever they would meet. Many of these young people came to faith in Christ and were delivered from drug, alcohol, or sex addictions, or from simply a life without purpose or direction.

During the Sunday school hour, I met a couple who shared their story. After leaving high school, they lived together in a tent on the beach. He surfed, while she sold jewelry she created from seashells to help buy food. One day, someone shared Christ with them.

After the Sunday school class ended, we all filed into the main sanctuary for corporate worship. I noticed this same couple standing down the row to my right. As the congregation began to sing "Amazing Grace," the rote lyrics rolled out of my mouth: "Amazing grace, how sweet the sound, that saved a wretch like me." But as this couple sang, tears were streaming down their faces. Why? They had just shared how wretched their lives were and how grateful they were to the One who changed everything. That is the power of worshipping from a heart of gratitude.

Gratitude is a fruit of remembering. Even though it had been years since this couple was lost, living a life of futility on the beach, they had the courage to remember from where they had come. The apostle Paul reminds us of exactly how wretched we were before we knew Christ. We were slaves of sin, children of darkness, deceived, tossed to and fro, enemies of

God (see Rom. 6:6; Eph. 5:8; 4:14; Rom. 5:10). But isn't that negative? Why bring up days gone by? Here's why: If remembering our wretched past causes us discomfort, we may be in danger of spiritual amnesia. Spiritual amnesia begets lack of gratitude. Lack of gratitude begets wallpaper worship.

SIMON SAYS, "DON'T BE LIKE ME"

Jesus' visit to Simon the Pharisee's home in Luke 7:36–47 is a bold illustration of how self-absorbed we can become when we choose not to remember or be grateful.

> One of the Pharisees asked him to eat with him, and he went into the Pharisee's house and reclined at table. And behold, a woman of the city, who was a sinner, when she learned that he was reclining at table in the Pharisee's house, brought an alabaster flask of ointment, and standing behind him at his feet, weeping, she began to wet his feet with her tears and wiped them with the hair of her head and kissed his feet and anointed them with the ointment. Now when the Pharisee who had invited him saw this, he said to himself, "If this man were a prophet, he would have known who and what sort of woman this is who is touching him, for she is a sinner." And Jesus answering said to him, "Simon, I have something to say to you." And he answered, "Say it, Teacher."

> "A certain moneylender had two debtors. One owed five hundred denarii, and the other fifty.

When they could not pay, he cancelled the debt of both. Now which of them will love him more?" Simon answered, "The one, I suppose, for whom he cancelled the larger debt." And he said to him, "You have judged rightly." Then turning toward the woman he said to Simon, "Do you see this woman? I entered your house; you gave me no water for my feet, but she has wet my feet with her tears and wiped them with her hair. You gave me no kiss, but from the time I came in she has not ceased to kiss my feet. You did not anoint my head with oil, but she has anointed my feet with ointment. Therefore I tell you, her sins, which are many, are forgiven— for she loved much. But he who is forgiven little, loves little.

The prostitute quietly wept as she broke her expensive vial to anoint the feet of the One who gave her dignity through forgiveness. The leper left his friends to run back, find Jesus, and fall at His feet to say thank you. The couple in church sang with tear-streaked faces because they remembered how wretched their lives were without knowing Jesus. Is the duty of worship really so taxing, so rote, so produced that we find ourselves in church, standing there, sipping coffee, passively observing like Simon the Pharisee? I am guilty. Are you?

THANKS FOR THE MIRACLES

As Jesus entered the city of Jerusalem riding on a donkey to the cheers of an adoring crowd, the Gospel of Luke records that the people were cheering because of the miracles they had seen.

> As he was drawing near—already on the way down the Mount of Olives—the whole multitude of his disciples began to rejoice and praise God with a loud voice for all the mighty works [miracles] that they had seen, saying, "Blessed is the King who comes in the name of the Lord! Peace in heaven and glory in the highest!" (Luke 19:37–38)

Perhaps some in that crowd had been around when Jesus spoke the word and the centurion's servant was healed. Maybe some had previously followed Jesus into the town of Nain and witnessed His raising the widow's dead son out of a coffin. Maybe a few more of those nine healed lepers were in the crowd cheering. Who knows? The passage is very clear: The people were praising and thanking God because of the miracles they had seen Jesus perform.

Have you seen miracles? Have your fellow worshippers seen any miracles? When was the last time you prayed a prayer and then saw a direct answer? Yesterday? Last week? Last year? Even once, in a galaxy far, far away in your life? Even then, if so, why do we settle for wallpaper worship?

WORSHIP'S TOUR OF DUTY

As the son of an air force chaplain, my childhood was marked by moving every three years to a different installation. From my first grade year until graduation from high school we moved five times. While I was in college, my parents moved twice more before retiring. Since 2001, deployments and temporary duty assignments (TDY) have increased exponentially, requiring many men and women in uniform to deploy seven or more times within a few years. As long as we are a nation, there will always be a military, so there will always be tours of duty. As long as there is life on this side of eternity, the Father's self-initiated search for true worshippers will continue. Someday, when all of time comes to a halt, perhaps God's search for worshippers will end. But worshipping itself will continue long into eternity. In other words, our tour of duty as worshippers never ends.

Imagine gathering every week with believers who understand the inheritance they have been given, who see their lives through a favored vantage point because they lived out their week—with all its trials or triumphs—from a perspective of privilege. Naturally, they feel compelled to gather for the purpose of lifting their voices together in gratitude because of the incredible meal God has spread on their behalf. Does your worship experience look like that? Duty has never been so sweet.

PART TWO:

WHAT WORSHIP ISN'T

6

WORSHIP ISN'T CASUAL

Worship, I say, rises or falls with our concept of God. . . .
If there is one terrible disease in the Church of Christ, it is that
we do not see God as great as He is. We're too familiar with God.
—A.W. Tozer, *Whatever Happened to Worship?*

After I graduated from college, I was figuring out how I was going to get to Nashville to pursue my dream. Meanwhile, there was an upcoming event called Washington for Jesus. Every state was being organized by voting districts to gather Christians for a huge rally to be held in Washington, DC for a day of prayer and fasting on behalf of the country. Since I had no immediate plans, I volunteered to be my state's youth coordinator.

I was given a list of churches to contact to schedule myself to speak and promote the event. The first was a large, young, up-and-coming church in the state. I spoke in their Sunday services and had lunch with the pastor and his wife. He offered me a job on the spot as the church youth pastor. I didn't know anything about youth ministry and was still dreaming of Nashville. But I felt strongly that I should accept. The three years I spent at that church taught me a boatload of lessons that I've never forgotten and gave me my first experience in the real world of megachurch ministry.

One such experience was when the senior staff decided to "beef up" the Sunday night service to get more people interested in coming. They hired an out-of-state music director who was known for his big choral arrangements and NBC Symphony Orchestra style band arrangements. Since all of the band charts had been used in other churches, his secretary hired union musicians who could read charts and play on cue. The music man simply flew into town each week and conducted the music for what became known as "Sunday Night Live." It worked. Crowds increased, offerings were up, and the senior pastor got his desire to preach one more time on Sundays.

One night, I slipped out of the service to get something from my office in the adjacent building. All of the hired musicians were taking a break during the sermon. They were outside smoking cigarettes and talking about sports, cars, women, and anything other than what was going on inside the sanctuary. These guys were union players enjoying a Sunday night gig. The complete disconnect between these musicians and the meaningful worship they were helping to facilitate was something I never forgot.

If you have worked on the inside of a church, either as a paid staffer or a volunteer, it is a sure bet you have your own stories of disintegration experienced both in programs as well as people. Throughout history, the church has no doubt had its dark moments since the very beginning. The point is not that there are negatives surrounding some of our worship experiences. Instead, the question is: How will we respond when negatives happen? If you're like me, you want to ignore the negatives instead of patiently and prayerfully figuring out how to lovingly confront them. I have heard many stories from frustrated churchgoers, as well as staffers, who are just gutting it out, praying God will change their own hearts, mainly because they feel helpless to do anything that will effect change in their particular situation. When is it a reflection of great character to hang in there in order to make a difference? And when is it wise to just walk away?

Worship takes on many forms and styles. Yet its function is always the same: to lead the people of God from their own minds, hearts, and experiences, into the mind, heart, and experience of God. Worship is a transcendent journey. Pastor and author Rick Warren says, "The heart of worship is surrender."[1] A spiritual experience in worship is far beyond any natural human experience. When we realize we are to be taken on a journey from the common to the holy, from the flesh to the spirit, from our presence to God's presence, the way in which we get there becomes very important. A common loaf of bread and a cup of wine, when designated for the service of worship, become extraordinary vessels that lead a worshipper into an experience far beyond the physical elements themselves. The common forms through which we worship transform into something greater, something holy.

Let's look at an instance where the leaders of corporate worship in Israel were so casual they became flippant about what they were doing. As we read the story of Aaron's sons in Leviticus, imagine these leaders sitting outside, smoking cigarettes, having a drink, and chewing the fat while God's manifest presence awaited them in the tent. What were the people gathering for worship thinking about their leaders? A more probing question would be: What was God thinking about these leaders?

> Now Nadab and Abihu, the sons of Aaron, took their respective firepans, and after putting fire in them, placed incense on it and offered strange fire before the LORD, which He had not commanded them. And fire came out from the presence of the LORD and consumed them, and they died before the LORD. Then Moses said to Aaron, "It is what the LORD spoke, saying,

'By those who come near Me I will be treated as holy,
And before all the people I will be honored'"

(Lev. 10:1–3, NASB).

Why is it that great men in ministry always try to bequeath their position to their sons? Sometimes there is an appropriate call of God to the offspring. Sometimes there is not. Nevertheless, it was the customary practice in ancient Israel to hand down the office within the bloodline of one's family. No doubt there have been sons throughout history who have carried their father's torches well. But there have been instances, like this one in Leviticus, when the sons in line for ministry were a failure and a disappointment. Let's consider the backstory.

Aaron, the first priest of Israel, had four sons, all being groomed into the priesthood after their father. The elder sons, Nadab and

Abihu, were alongside their dad and Moses in the literal presence of the Lord. God tells Moses to fit priestly garments for Aaron and his sons in Exodus 28. Their job was to minister, not to the people, but to God Himself. Nadab and Abihu are not mentioned again until this story in Leviticus 10. We can only assume that they were ministering to the Lord alongside their father Aaron, until this fateful day. Something happened along the way to these young men. With all they had experienced, why would they take their priestly vessels and offer a strange incense before the Lord, which "He had not commanded them"? Why, after all their training in the office of the priest and all the holy moments they had observed while being mentored, would these two brothers do something so casual and flippant?

> The LORD then spoke to Aaron, saying, "Do not drink wine or strong drink, neither you nor your sons with you, when you come into the tent of meeting, so that you will not die—it is a perpetual statute throughout your generations—and so as to make a distinction between the holy and the profane, and between the unclean and the clean." (10:8–10, NASB)

This story gives us a number of lesson points: (1) Don't lead in worship if you are inebriated, (2) tempting God to see what He might do in response to your sacrilege is not a good idea, and (3) God sees a difference between the holy and the profane.

Aaron's sons' job description was not about entertaining crowds or leading worshippers into some kind of feel-good experience. Their duties were to minister to God. But they had actually entered the holy place of ministry so intoxicated that together they had the brave idea to offer a strange incense in their firepans just to see what would happen.

Why would a priest—a man set aside to minister solely to the Lord—do such a thing? We don't know what caused these elder sons of Aaron to be drinking heavily or how long they conspired to enter the Holy Place and pull their boneheaded stunt. In our world, it is highly unlikely that an up-front church staff member would take to the platform or pulpit on a given Sunday, drunk out of their senses. Perhaps the more relevant issue to consider is this: What are we drunk with? As a leader of worship or a lay worshipper ministering before the Lord, what are you "drinking" during the week that causes you to be divided or disconnected? What are you allowing in your life that you are taking to the platform of ministry that the Lord Himself would look down on as profane? Is it an unbiblical relationship in your life? An addiction you can't lose? Envy? Dualistic behavior? Are you living two separate lives, one during the week and another at church?

A wise yet difficult exercise would be to sit down and honestly make a list of those things in your life as a leader, a worshipper, that God would call profane and unholy. You may ask: And do what with it? Put it on Facebook? Of course not. There is healing promised in James 5:16: "Confess your sins to one another and pray for one another, that you may be healed." Living in isolation is what puts us in danger. Isolating the stuff we need to bring into the light is isolating the isolation. I know, I've been there. Especially when others are looking to me for spiritual leadership. If we choose to hide, we are not only contributing to the leadership problem of the church, we become the problem. The only way to healing is through the confidence of a close and trusted friend. So, go ahead. Make the list. Take it to prayer with someone that you trust implicitly. But that "someone" needs to be someone who will be honest with you about seeking your healing by providing clear direction. My personal list (yes, I've done it) provides a way to track my awareness of God's healing in me, and my progress toward victory in vulnerable areas. Quite honestly, the list will grow as our maturity grows. The closer we get to God, the more we realize our flesh is not like Him at all. The more of Him we see, the more aware of our fallenness we become. It can be taxing emotionally, but it is worth the journey. What other choice is there?

Whether we choose to face it or not, the vices that those of us in ministry try desperately to hide put us in the camp of Nadab and Abihu. Their lives went down in history for ending at the point of their weakest and most foolish moment. They had served alongside their father, Aaron, in the office of the priesthood for many years. In spite of years of loyal service to the Lord and the people of Israel, they are remembered only for their folly.

It is important to understand that God considers the gap between that which is holy and that which is profane to be wide and deep. We who carry His name must share His view and be as appalled as He is at how narrow the gap between the holy and profane can be in our own lives. This is an especially important attribute for leaders to grasp. James 3:1 says, "Let not many *of you* become teachers, my brethren, knowing that as such we will incur a stricter judgment" (NASB). There have been times in my career as a musical worship leader that I have not felt fit for the platform. For instance, right before I am supposed to lead a worship gathering, Angela and I have an argument which does not resolve. She is in tears and I am angry—but oops, look at the clock: "Sorry honey—I gotta go to the church to lead worship." Or even worse, I remember times I was flippant about sin; I failed to honor God with my eyes, or my tongue, or my mind. I move on, in denial that God's grace is license for me to sin (see Rom. 6:1–2). It's systemic in all of us, in our flesh. I have learned and am still learning that the flesh is not something I manage; I am supposed to kill it. Paul's words in Galatians 2:20 speak directly to my own heart: "I have been crucified with Christ. It is no longer I who live, but Christ who lives in me. And the life I now live in the flesh I live by faith in the Son of God, who loved me and gave himself for me." He is saying, "Sure we live in the flesh; there's no way around it on this side of eternity. The difference between victory or defeat is living in the flesh by faith."

Perhaps there are too many people in positions of leadership who should not be there. I can honestly say I have been one of those. There are some in positions of leadership simply because they have abilities in speaking or music that fit well on a platform or stage. Don Chapman, a writer for *Worship Leader* magazine, posted an article that spoke to a phenomenon he called Rock Star Worship Leaders (RSWL).[2]

> A friend of mine is using a church job-placement agency to find a worship leader position for himself. The representative mentioned they've never had so many worship leader job openings. When asked

why, the representative explained that churches are finding the performance worship leader thing isn't working out so well. It seems congregations are tired of being performed to instead of led in worship.

The job my friend found is with a megachurch who just fired their own RSWL. This guy hopped around stage during worship, trying to drum up enthusiasm like any good rock star would in concert.

As my friend looked at the RSWL's set list from the past six weeks, he noticed *not a single song was repeated*. Typical RSWL behavior—they're performing worship songs, not leading them.

One big reason my friend's church fired their RSWL was that they were concerned their congregation wasn't worshipping during the music.

The story of Nadab and Abihu warns us that even though some are trained for leadership, training does not necessarily mean they are gifted for it. The heart of a godly leader will be evident, even when the leader's gifts may not be as polished as another's. Remember the old woman in Luke who stood in the offering line and gave her two copper coins as the wealthy threw in bags of money from their surplus of riches (see 21:1–4). Jesus' attention was on the poorly dressed old woman and not the well-dressed wealthy.

We will delve into more detail on overcasualizing the worship experience in the chapter titled "Three Things Missed in

Contemporary Worship" and its counterpart on traditional worship ("Three Things Missed in Traditional Worship"). For now, it is relevant to consider: Has my experience as a worshipper or a leader become casual or even flippant? How has that happened? Do I not understand the difference between the holy and the profane? Am I drunk with something else in my life that is keeping me from experiencing God's presence when I gather for worship? Is private, intimate worship something I avoid and, if so, why?

Pastor A. W. Tozer has become a much-quoted author, long after his death in 1963. Tozer never attended seminary, but pastored churches with the Christian and Missionary Alliance denomination for forty-four years. In his book *Whatever Happened to Worship?*, Tozer wrote, "Worship, I say, rises or falls with our concept of God. . . . If there is one terrible disease in the Church of Christ, it is that we do not see God as great as He is. We're too familiar with God."[3] Tozer was speaking in the context of a Protestant evangelical movement in 1950s America. The message of salvation had become so familiar that it had become formulated into a casual method of relationship with a God who no longer held a place of reverence, but convenience. For many who lived during that era, being a Christian was synonymous with being an American. We see this casual attitude in today's churches as well. It finds its expression through an attitude that exudes, "Jesus is my homeboy." Or in songs that are difficult to differentiate who the lyrics are addressing: my wife, my boyfriend, my lover, or God Almighty and His incarnate Son?

In the last chapter, we looked at Simon the Pharisee and the prostitute who broke the vial of perfume on Jesus' feet.

Consider this: Simon the Pharisee wore fine linen robes and gold rings; he lived in a nice home with servants to bring him dinner. He was a leader, a teacher, an expert in the law. But in his heart, he was a dry well. Somewhere in his religious duties he forgot that, without God's mercy, grace, and redemption, he himself was that sinful woman on the floor in need of Jesus' mercy and forgiveness. At some point, he had forgotten the depth of his need, resulting in a casual flippancy in his faith, even to the point of belittling this woman's acts of worship, which Jesus recognized as true.

THE NAME OF JESUS: COMMON OR EXTRAORDINARY?

Recently, my wife and I decided to attend a local megachurch we had not yet visited in our community. It was early December and we were curious to find out how a church of this size was recognizing the upcoming Christmas season. We arrived late that morning and the sermon was already well under way. As we parked and got out to walk to the front door, we could hear the sermon as it was being broadcast over loudspeakers in the parking lot. The person speaking was describing the shepherds watching their flocks in the field on the night of the angel's appearance. "Those shepherds weren't just afraid when that angel appeared. It scared the bejesus out of 'em!" We stopped in the parking lot in disbelief. We couldn't believe what we had just heard. Here we were going into a service to worship the King of Kings and Lord of Lords, and His name was thrown out like a used banana peel. My first thought was, what are the children in the service thinking?

My second was, I wonder when they will do a series on the power of the name of Jesus. (My last thought came when we were leaving the service and 80 percent of the congregants were standing there, not singing, but watching the band perform the last set of songs for them.)

The gospel is so accessible that concepts such as "atonement for sin" are not only foreign, but unwelcome so as to not scare off the unchurched. We have so casualized God, it is no wonder that people do not understand the difference between the holy and the profane. Many of us in leadership have blurred that line in our life example.

TRAINING VS. WARFARE

I was mentored for sixteeen years by retired Marine Lieutenant Colonel Tom Hemingway. I met Tom in 1985 when I took a six-month break from my music career by living and working at a Christian camp high in the Rocky Mountains. The camp/conference center, called Spring Canyon, was owned and operated as a ministry of Officers Christian Fellowship, an international ministry to military leaders and their families. Tom, as a retired marine, was the camp director. He used to tell a story about a time when he was teaching reconnaissance to a platoon at Camp Pendleton, California. They would come to his class to learn the basic concepts of patrolling, scouting, and regrouping at a common geographical point. Since the class was always scheduled after lunch, much of the instruction was lost as the marines would fall into a confused slumber. But when that same group of marines was instructed to go into a live fire combat theater, suddenly everyone was paying very close attention to the concepts they were learning in their training class back at Camp Pendleton. Same marines, same instructional materials, same concepts. What was the difference? One was training and the other warfare. One was casual, the other was serious.

If our worship seems so casual that it has become flippant, it is a sign that we are trapped in a training mentality. Paul tells Timothy that there are those in the church who are "always learning and never able to arrive at a knowledge of the truth" (2 Tim. 3:7). These are the churched, religious people who remain in a training mentality and never make the switch to real warfare. In other words, what we know in Christ—that which brings us to a place of worship—is not real. It is hypothetical. It is mental assent. It is simply training information that may come in handy someday. A training mentality results in a flippant, casual worship experience.

On the other hand, there are others who gather for worship who share a sense that they are living in a spiritual battlefield. Live ammunition is being fired at the souls of those around them. They take in every instruction, knowing that it will be used in the here and now. They are sharp, attentive, and possess a sense of urgency about their spirituality. Their experience in worship is anything but flippant or casual. They take worship very seriously, knowing, in humility, that it is a privilege to be a child of God. They know this means that they are also a soldier for Christ, engaged in a very real battle for the souls of people. They have switched from a training mentality to a warfare mentality.

In wanting to be one of those who have switched from training to warfare, there are two things my mentor made clear to me.

First of all spiritual warfare (not unlike conventional warfare) is fought alongside other soldiers. Those who choose to "go it alone" will not succeed. It is impossible to fight battles alone. Again, James 5:14–16 speaks to the team effort it takes to fight the spiritual as well as physical battles in our lives.

> Is anyone among you sick? Let him call for the elders of the church, and let them pray over him, anointing him with oil in the name of the Lord. And the prayer of faith will save the one who is sick, and the Lord will raise him up. And if he has committed sins, he will be forgiven. Therefore, confess your sins to one another and pray for one another, that you may be healed. The prayer of a righteous person has great power as it is working.

Even though this passage is often used for those who are physically sick and in need of healing, it is also useful for those who are sick in other ways—through sin or habits or selfishness or addictions. The concept of a "band of brothers or sisters" is very clear in verse 14: "Call for the elders." Pick up the phone and call two or three persons you consider confidants—maybe leaders in your church family—and ask for prayer and support. Getting healthy in every way is not something we try to do in isolation. Verse 16 goes a step further. Confessing sin is also done with "one another." Warfare is only successful when it is fought with a platoon, a team, or even a company of fellow soldiers. The problem for some of us is that we are scared of revealing ourselves to others. However, if the enemy can isolate us, he can take us out completely. War is never won by one soldier; it is fought and won by soldiers—plural. (See also Heb. 10:24–25; Prov. 11:14; Eccles. 4:9–10; Gal. 6:1–2.)

Secondly, when called upon, we may have to lay our own lives down for someone. Jesus makes a statement in John 15:13 that is a staple of our Christian faith: "Greater love has no one than this, that someone lay down his life for his friends." There are many war stories of soldiers making the ultimate sacrifice of their lives in order to save the lives of their battlefield buddies. In spiritual warfare, laying down our life for a friend may mean giving up our life, but for two minutes at a time.

What does it look like to lay down my life two minutes at a time? Perhaps it means laying down my time to listen to my neighbor's story; being emotionally available to my spouse and children, so they know, beyond any doubt, that their importance in my life is not merely a concept but a reality; or taking a few minutes to clean up someone else's mess at a church or social function. When in a *training mentality,* I may skip over the opportunities God brings into my life to lay down my time for someone else. In a training mentality, my agenda, my appointments, my schedule are more important to me than another's need. But a *warfare mentality* translates into actually listening instead of talking; engaging instead of isolating; holding my tongue when my instinct is to lash out. A warfare mentality means I understand that there is something eternal going on—not just what I can see at a given moment. It is the acute awareness that God is always at work in us "both to will and to work for his good pleasure" (Phil. 2:13).

SPONTANEITY VS. INTENTIONALITY

There are traditions within evangelicalism that consider worship to be something that is never planned, but entirely spontaneous. In fact, the more spontaneous the worship experience, the more spiritual it is considered to be. I have attended many services from that tradition, and have had wonderful experiences and gained valuable insights. However, the New Testament church in Corinth was a body that operated under the spirit of "anything goes" and everything went! The idea of corporate worship being something intentional but also open to spontaneity is something the apostle Paul lays out clearly.

> What is the outcome then, brethren? When you assemble, each one has a psalm, has a teaching, has a revelation, has a tongue, has an interpretation. Let all things be done for edification; . . . for God is not a God of confusion but of peace, as in all the churches of the saints. . . . But all things must be done properly and in an orderly manner. (1 Cor. 14:26, 33, 40, NASB)

Even within the public practice of spiritual gifts of the Holy Spirit, Paul offered guidelines to help steer them from becoming flippant about their order in worship and laid out the how-tos—so that in freedom there is order, and in order there is corporate edification. Perhaps it was Paul's way of helping the New Testament church avoid falling into wallpaper worship that becomes so casual it results in flippancy, even when the gifts of the Spirit are at work.

A MESSAGE TO LEADERS

There is much talk these days of "integrity in leadership." When leaders fall, it affects us all. Paul understood this. In Romans he wrote, "You who say 'don't steal,' do you steal?" (see 2:21). If I am finding my worship immobilized because I am flippant, casual, jumping between the holy and the profane without conviction, trapped in a training mentality and not able to make the switch to a warfare mentality, or inebriated with an addiction I cannot break, I need to ask myself some tough personal questions. Even though I may be familiar with God and exposed to the church, its language, its lingo, its ways and means of doing things, I have to ask myself:

- Do I possess an "appearance of godliness," but deny its power? (2 Tim. 3:5)
- Am I not repelled by the profane? Does it hold me captive to curiosity like Nadab and Abihu?
- Am I annoyed by these questions?

A "yes" answer to any of these three questions may indicate that a God-initiated spirituality may not exist in you. If this is you, you are probably in one of two categories:

1. You are attending church on the weekends, but you find there is no power to live the other days of the week. Your life does not reflect God's difference between the holy and the profane. Attending church is a ritual for you that you hope will produce some luck in your life for things to go better for you.

2. If you are a leader in church, you find the role exhausting
   because it drains you of energy, leaving you feeling power-
   less and disheartened. Your church leadership has become
   no different from your career work the rest of the week.
   Like Nadab and Abihu, you lead in a state of "drunkenness"
   because something in your life is sapping your strength and
   your good judgment. And worse, you cannot seem to let go
   of it. You do not possess the power of the godliness about
   which you sing or teach. It seems good for others but never
   good enough for you. You are trapped. Now is the time to
   adopt God's standards of the difference between the holy
   and the profane. Now is the time to get clean. It was too
   late for the sons of Aaron after they had been consumed by
   God's fire. Don't wait to be burned before getting clean.

My friend, it is never too late to bring the confusion of the
holy and the profane to God. It is never too late to confront our
compromise, denial, and emptiness before God. Let Him take
them from you through His power and His Word. God will
remove it and replace your emptiness with the fullness of His
Spirit. Learning from the foolish mistake of Nadab and Abihu,
you must bring all of this emptiness to Him in complete humility and brokenness. Admit you are worthless without His power. But you must bring your situation to God in the confidence
of fellow soldiers, not alone. You cannot repent and get clean in
isolation (see James 5:16). Like the old woman giving her copper coins, you must give 100 percent of your deeds over to Him
in exchange for 100 percent of His love, forgiveness, acceptance,
and empowerment. This is the gospel, the good news. It is about
exchanging what you have for what only He can provide.

If you answered "yes" to any of the three questions previously listed, you are leading a lifestyle that God never intended for you. His intention is to save you from the futility of flippancy and to redeem your heart, your gifts, your deeds, your motives, your behaviors into something that actually looks like Him. Only then can you truly lead others into the holiness you are experiencing for yourself.

Start here, start now, and let Him write a new story for you—with His power inside of you as the center of that story. This is what Jesus meant when He said the Father is seeking worshippers (and leaders of worship) who will worship Him in spirit and in truth.

7

WORSHIP ISN'T DEEDS

*It takes many good deeds to build a good reputation, and only one
bad one to lose it.*

—Benjamin Franklin

*If anyone is a hearer of the word and not a doer, he is like a man
who looks intently at his natural face in a mirror. For he looks at
himself and goes away and at once forgets what he was like.*

James 1:23–24

The great reformer Martin Luther had such a bad taste
in his mouth from the church doctrine of earning favor
with God through deeds, that he protested the inclusion of the letter of James in the New Testament Canon because he felt it was too works oriented. In many ways, Luther's
concern is understandable, especially if one comes from a family
or a church that emphasizes deeds as a means to grace.

When we think of worship in an overall application, it describes the very expression of every area of the believer's life.

All the things that we do—work, family, marriage, parenting, ministry, friendship—become expressions of the depth of our faith. Therefore, it seems logical to say that each area of our lives can be an expression of worship. But the Scriptures also teach that doing something in the name of Christ does not automatically make that deed an action of worship.

The Bible is full of stories of people who failed at making the distinction between which of their deeds expressed faith and which expressed a lack of faith. Contrastingly, there are other Bible characters who fully understood how their deeds pleased God and were acceptable acts of worship. We will examine one of each. The first character we will examine, King Saul, loudly justified his wrong deeds as being an act of worship. The second character we will examine, a poor widow, silently committed a deed that will forever be recognized as an act of worshipping in spirit and in truth.

KING SAUL, WHO BLEW IT ALL

The story of King Saul in First Samuel 15 is one of the saddest stories of the Old Testament. But don't skip this part! To be able to learn from a leader's mistakes gives us a perspective of privilege that can teach us at whatever level in life we find ourselves. Big corporations pay hundreds of thousands of dollars to teach their executives and employees the kind of principles we can hear and learn in this classic story. So buckle up, and put your tray in its upright and locked position. Here we go!

> And Samuel said to Saul, "The LORD sent me
> to anoint you king over his people Israel; now

therefore listen to the words of the LORD. Thus says the LORD of hosts, 'I have noted what Amalek did to Israel in opposing them on the way when they came up out of Egypt. Now go and strike Amalek and devote to destruction all that they have. Do not spare them, but kill both man and woman, child and infant, ox and sheep, camel and donkey.'"...

And Saul defeated the Amalekites from Havilah as far as Shur, which is east of Egypt. And he took Agag the king of the Amalekites alive and devoted to destruction all the people with the edge of the sword. But Saul and the people spared Agag and the best of the sheep and of the oxen and of the fattened calves and the lambs, and all that was good, and would not utterly destroy them. All that was despised and worthless they devoted to destruction.

The word of the LORD came to Samuel: "I regret that I have made Saul king, for he has turned back from following me and has not performed my commandments." And Samuel was angry, and he cried to the LORD all night. And Samuel rose early to meet Saul in the morning. And it was told Samuel, "Saul came to Carmel, and behold, he set up a monument for himself and turned and passed on and went down to Gilgal." And Samuel came to Saul, and Saul said to him, "Blessed be you to the LORD. I have performed the commandment of the LORD." And Samuel said, "What then is this bleating of the sheep in my ears and the lowing of the oxen that I hear?" Saul said, "They have brought them from the Amalekites, for the people spared the best of the sheep and of the oxen to sacrifice to the LORD your God, and the rest we have devoted to destruction." Then Samuel said to Saul, "Stop! I will tell you what the LORD said to me this night." And he said to him, "Speak."

And Samuel said, "Though you are little in your own eyes, are you not the head of the tribes of Israel? The LORD anointed you king over Israel. And the LORD sent you on a mission and said, 'Go, devote to destruction the sinners, the Amalekites, and fight against them until they are consumed.' Why then did you not obey the voice of the LORD? Why did you pounce on the spoil and do what was evil in the sight of the LORD?" And Saul said to Samuel, "I have obeyed the voice of the LORD. I have gone on the mission on which the LORD sent me. I have brought Agag the king of Amalek, and I have devoted the Amalekites to destruction. But the people took of the spoil, sheep and oxen, the best of the things devoted to destruction, to sacrifice to the LORD your God in Gilgal." And Samuel said,

"Has the LORD as great delight in burnt offerings and sacrifices,
    as in obeying the voice of the LORD?
Behold, to obey is better than sacrifice,
    and to listen than the fat of rams.

For rebellion is as the sin of divination,
  and presumption is as iniquity and idolatry.
Because you have rejected the word of the LORD,
  he has also rejected you from being king."

(1 Sam. 15:1–3, 7–23)

Whew! There are so many violations of good leadership principles in this story that it would take a separate book to extrapolate them all. So let's synthesize and simplify.

TWO MEN OF GOD, TWO AGENDAS

Like most rulers of early Israel, King Saul was given Samuel the prophet to guide him, intercede for him, and keep him accountable to God's purposes and future for the nation. Saul's orders from God, through His prophet Samuel, were clear: "Attack and totally destroy them and all that belongs to them." Surely the king had other advisors in addition to the prophet Samuel. Perhaps these other advisors counseled him that to annihilate the Amalekites may not give the impression of a "kinder, gentler" king of Israel. We don't know. We do know that Saul feared what his own people thought (see 15:24) and chose to listen to their voice instead of obeying God's command. So after the battle, Saul spared King Agag and the best of the livestock, and then proclaimed to have done it all "in the name of the Lord."

This story shines a white-hot spotlight on the stage of obedience. In his rebuke of King Saul, Samuel makes a statement that we can apply to worship: "Has the LORD as great delight in burnt offerings and sacrifices, / as in obeying the voice of the LORD? / Behold, to obey is better than sacrifice, / and to listen than the fat of rams" (1 Sam. 15:22). In our application, does the Lord delight as much in our forms of worship (songs, readings, liturgies, programs, cantatas, instrumentation, sound, staging, lighting) as in our being obedient to His commands for us? Nope! Compared to obedience to His commands, our forms of worship mean nothing to God. In other words, God will take obedience to His commands over our forms of worship every time. This is consistent throughout the Old and New Testaments, and God has shown His commitment to this principle throughout church history.

The consequences of Saul's blatant compromise—and even worse, his rationalization—are devastating. Later, in verses 25 and 30, he begs to be pardoned for what he has done. But Samuel makes it clear that God will not allow Saul to stay in the position of leadership and authority He had put him in. Samuel tells Saul, "The LORD has torn the kingdom of Israel from you this day and has given it to a neighbor of yours, who is better than you" (15:28). Ouch!

According to Saul, he spared the livestock so the people of Israel would have animals to sacrifice in their ritual of worship. To God, Saul's deed and rationalization were akin to Adam's classic blame game in Genesis 3 after eating the forbidden fruit. Remember that conversation?

God: "Have you eaten of the tree of which I commanded you not to eat?"

Adam: "The woman whom you gave to be with me, she gave me fruit of the tree, and I ate."

Apparently, obedience—not deeds—is paramount to God. Saul's "acts of worship" were a noisy gong to the ears of his God. Our actions, even when they're performed in the name of the Lord, are not necessarily acts of worship. We may want them to be, but wanting does not make them so.

A LITTLE BECOMES A LOT

The late NCAA championship basketball coach John Wooden said, "It's the little details that are vital. Little things make big things happen." How is it that the little things are those that, for the most part, go unnoticed? When added up, little things become a series of choices that have positive or negative consequences. Wooden understood this principle when it came to coaching the basketball team at UCLA. Apparently all the little things he coached his players to do in the privacy of the practice gym, with no audience watching, paid off. Under his direction, Wooden's team won the NCAA basketball national championship title ten times out of his twelve seasons as head coach. The championship trophies on display at UCLA are simply an affirmation that what Coach Wooden believed was what Jesus said two thousand years prior to college basketball: "One who is faithful in a very little is also faithful in much" (Luke 16:10).

When we are tasked with a job, the person who gave us that job expects us to do it right, all the way down to the moments when no one else is watching. In my experiences of preparing a talk, rehearsing music, or even paying my bills, the principle of being faithful in the little details translates into success in the larger ones. This means each deed I do faithfully, with excellence, and in obedience to God's will, can be considered an act of worship. The results can be powerful and stand the test of time. The widow in Luke 21:1–4 exemplified doing something small that became something eternal.

> Jesus looked up and saw the rich putting their gifts into the offering box, and he saw a poor widow put in two small copper coins. And he said, "Truly, I tell you, this poor widow has put in more than all of them. For they all contributed out of their abundance, but she out of her poverty put in all she had to live on."

As we discuss "when deeds become an act of worship," let's break this story down a bit so we can get our minds around it.

Jesus and His disciples have arrived in Jerusalem and decide to visit the Temple. They arrive when the parishioners are standing in line to give their offerings for the temple treasury. Standing in that line are the rich folks of the Jewish community. We know this from the text, but we have to imagine that Luke mentions they are rich because the people in line looked rich! Imagine successful businessmen with their spouses bringing their cash to pour into the treasury urn. Perhaps their clothing, jewelry, and large purses full of coins gave them away. The ladies smelled of ointments and pleasant scents, with gold chains hanging from their hair and bracelets dangling, as they looked the part of the rich man's spouse. Perhaps the conversations overheard between the men were about commerce and trade. Whatever the scene, picture Jesus arriving with His twelve motley disciples, most of whom were blue-collar fishermen in common clothing, fresh from their journey on the dusty Judean roads.

Most of the disciples had spent their lives either in construction or at sea in the fishing industry. If you've ever seen *The Perfect Storm* starring George Clooney and Mark

Wahlberg, you have a fair example of the lifestyle these fishermen lived. Their wives didn't dress like the wives of the rich men they saw in the offering line that day. They themselves perhaps had never smelled the fragrances of rich women or ever worn the clothing of successful businessmen. When each rich person lifted their bag of coins to dump their offering into the temple treasury, the noise of the pouring coins was like the sound of a wind tunnel. The eyes of the disciples probably bugged out. The conversation among them may have been something like this:

> "So that's how the other side lives!"

> "I've never seen so much money."

> "Never made that much wealth in all my years in the fishing business."

Just then, as the disciples may have been in their usual "talk amongst themselves" mode, Jesus took notice. And here's what happened as recorded by Luke.

> Jesus looked up and saw the rich putting their gifts into the offering box, and he saw a poor widow put in two small copper coins. And he said, "Truly, I tell you, this poor widow has put in more than all of them. For they all contributed out of their abundance, but she out of her poverty put in all she had to live on." (Luke 21:1–4)

In all the activity of the moment, Jesus is watching someone very out of place in this line of rich people. At the end of the line stands a poor widow. He knows she is poor because she looks poor. Her clothes are dirty, old, and ragged from years of being worn over and over again. She has no jewelry. She doesn't smell of fine fragrances. She clutches a small coin purse closely to her breast. As she stands a slight distance from the others in the line, Jesus notices as she finally reaches the offering urn for her turn to give into the treasury. She reaches into her purse and pulls out two small copper coins. Plink. Plink. They drop into the urn, on top of a mountain of gold coins.

As the disciples continue to gawk at the sheer wealth parading in front of them, Jesus suddenly yells out to them, "Look! Look at that! Did you see that?"

"I know," said Peter. "Bet you never saw so much money in the carpentry business in Nazareth."

Jesus answers with excitement. "You are right! This old widow just gave 100 percent of her wealth to the treasury. No one else in line before her got even close to that percentage. She wins!"

The disciples stop talking and stare at Jesus. He continues: "They all gave out of their surplus, but this widow gave everything she had to live on. This is amazing. This is an act of worship, and my Father is so pleased with her!"

The abandonment, sacrifice, trust, and faith that her deed required was worth more than all of the rest of the rich people's wealth combined. Her deed was noted forever in this story as extraordinary: a deed which was an act of worshipping in spirit and in truth.

The money of the rich, which represented a very slight portion of their possessions, seems equivalent to King Saul's rationalizations: "I *did* do what the Lord asked" said Saul (see 1 Sam. 15:20). "I *did* give to the treasury today," the rich people at the Temple in Luke 21 might have said. Saul's and the rich people's deeds may have had some kind of grandiose meaning in their own eyes. They thought they were worshipping. But in God's eyes, their deeds were to be ignored, as wallpaper hanging in a room.

What about what *we* call worship? If Jesus were to come to our worship service to observe like He did that day at the Temple, would He ignore what we are doing like He ignored the rich giving their offerings? Perhaps He is looking for something we are not. Perhaps we are more like the disciples, enamored with our own wealth of technical gear and talent. In the story of the widow, Jesus remains silent, until He sees the real thing pass by. What would He see in your church?

What act of obedience has the Lord asked of us? What has He whispered to us to give up to Him? How has He asked us to trust Him? What deed do we need to do to show Him we will obey Him? Which of our deeds is an act of worship? What deed have we heard His voice tell us to do, but we have postponed doing?

COMPASSION: THE RIGHT REACTION

Author and professor Tony Campolo came to our home church in Colorado to speak at a family retreat. In one of his talks, he began to criticize those who made choices like buying an expensive BMW or Mercedes, but had never sponsored a needy child through Compassion International for $39 a month. Angela and I didn't own a BMW or Mercedes, but Tony's point was clear to us. We had not given even a small portion of our income to help a child in need. His point pricked our hearts that night and we immediately signed up to be sponsors. That was an act of worship—not because $39 was all the money we had, but because it was a deed of obedience. We knew what we heard from Campolo's words that day were consistent with James 2:15–17: "If a brother or sister is poorly clothed and lacking in daily food, and one of you says to them, 'Go in peace, be warmed and filled,' without giving them the things needed for the body, what good is that? So also faith by itself, if it does not have works, is dead." We didn't need to pray for a week to know we needed to sponsor a child. We knew we had the money. We just needed to obey. "To obey is better than sacrifice" (1 Sam. 15:22).

Church history is full of deeds done in the name of the Lord that were blatant disobedience to His stated will: the Crusades, the Inquisition, the deadly riots following the Reformation, the Thirty Years War. Even Hitler's takeover of Germany in the 1930s was touted as "God's blessing for Germany." In recent times, the compromises of those in religious leadership are nauseating to a world desperate for leaders of integrity. The Academy Award for Best Picture in 2015 went to *Spotlight*, a movie based on the true story of child sex abuse covered up by the Catholic Church for decades. Christians' missteps have become fodder for late night comedy shows. And we wonder why the Christian church has little credibility? We are confounded as to why our neighbors won't come to church when we spend so much time and money to make it look, sound, and feel like a show they would relate to. They may be impressed with our production capabilities but that's not enough to make Joe Neighbor get out of bed and attend church. They can find slick production on their smart phones any day of the week.

To equate worship with deeds is risky. To equate worship with music is even riskier. Will we give them something different? Something real? Something other than wallpaper?

8

WORSHIP ISN'T MUSIC

Never teach a pig to sing. It hurts your ears and frustrates the pig.
—My college voice teacher

Worship and music. These two words fit together like milk and cookies, or peanut butter and jelly, or hot dogs and baseball, or fish and chips, or finely finished tongue and groove panels. Even so, they are not one and the same. Though they can work together to create something spiritually artistic and intimately personal, they find their identities separate from each other. Given our propensity to redefine words and phrases, we are at risk of using worship and music synonymously—and in so doing, outside biblical context. As mentioned in chapter 1, the twenty-first-century church has redefined worship and made it synonymous with a particular style of music, a song form within music, or even the effect that music has on us.

The Scriptures do not give us a definition of worship, but they do give us scores of examples of worship in action. One of the earliest biblical references to musical song is found in Exodus 15, where Moses' sister Miriam leads the Hebrew people in a song of praise to God after they have come through the Red Sea and witnessed their Egyptian captors' defeat. In this passage, forms of instrumentation (tambourines) and artistic motion (dancing) come together to create a musical expression of worship that was uniquely Hebrew and possibly new to a culture of people who had been enslaved for four hundred years. But whether it was a new or established mode of expression, the song of Moses was likely participated in by the majority of the Hebrews who were present. Given the exuberance of the moment, it is doubtful this was a solo performance by Miriam that the others passively observed.

The song of Deborah, found in Judges 5, is also one of the earliest song lyrics recorded in Scripture. Interestingly, the maiden Jael, who killed the enemy King Sisera by driving a tent peg into his skull while he was asleep in her tent after abandoning his own army (see 4:12–22), is celebrated in Deborah's song. (There's a worship lyric for ya!) First Samuel 2 records the song of Hannah, the prophet Samuel's mother. Though we have no reference to melodies, these songs were included in these historical texts as significant expressions of worshipping God for His delivering Israel from her enemies as well as delivering a son to a barren woman. Let's look at some biblical passages that separate the concepts of worship and music.

CELEBRATION OR SOLEMNITY

The prophet Amos expresses God's own words, in which the divine nomenclature makes it clear that music performed in a setting of worship does not automatically mean that worship is taking place.

> I hate, I despise your feasts,
>   and I take no delight in your solemn assemblies.
> Even though you offer me your burnt offerings and grain offerings,
>   I will not accept them;
> and the peace offerings of your fattened animals,
>   I will not look upon them.
> Take away from me the noise of your songs;
>   to the melody of your harps I will not listen.
> But let justice roll down like waters,
>   and righteousness like an ever-flowing stream.
>
> (Amos 5:21–24)

In this passage, God refers to songs sung and instruments played, as well as other nonmusical acts of worship, as an abhorrence. He turns a blind eye to His own required sacrifices of burnt offerings, grain offerings, and peace offerings. This passage is soberly clear that music, even when it is intended for worship, is worthless to God when it is not accompanied by righteous behavior outside of the worship service. Perhaps this is what Jesus meant when He said the Father seeks worshippers who worship Him in spirit and in truth (see John 4:23). From this passage in Amos, truth of the heart expressed through behavior is God's prerequisite to expressing devotion to Him through music. All the worship gatherings of celebration and praise (festivals) or in quiet solemnity (solemn assemblies) were simply wallpaper hanging to create a false context. The music meant nothing to God when His people were not practicing the very things they were singing about: righteousness and justice.

Those of us who plan worship services of quiet devotion err when we think that the more solemn the occasion the more of God's presence we will encounter. Likewise there are times we plan huge events with high volume and energy, thinking that God's presence and blessing is accessed through more demonstrative styles of corporate expression. Sheer volume or quiet tears can be appropriate, but according to this passage they are not worship. God's words through the prophet Amos clearly communicate that neither avenue of expression (solemn or celebratory) is right or appropriate when the worshippers are treating others badly in their families, workplaces, relationships, or communities. Clearly, these issues of justice and righteousness reign supreme in the heart of God, leaving our corporate worship experience to follow; not the other way around.

AS MEANINGLESS AS THE VOICE

In the Amos passage, God's words are focused on the people of Israel. In Ezekiel 33, God is speaking directly to Ezekiel—a personal conversation between the prophet and God Himself. God's words to Ezekiel are indicative of how God separates music from worship.

My people come to you, as they usually do, and sit before you to hear your words, but they do not put them into practice. Their mouths speak of love, but their hearts are greedy for unjust gain. Indeed, to them you are nothing more than one who sings love songs with a beautiful voice and plays an instrument well, for they hear your words but do not put them into practice.

When all this comes true—and it surely will—then they will know that a prophet has been among them. (Ezek. 33: 31–33, NIV)

Similar to Amos, God is clear here that what matters to Him is the obedience of the people to the principles He wants them to follow. When their hearts are "greedy for unjust gain" (33:31) their music offered to Him becomes equivalent to worthless noise. Their worship of Him is simply wallpaper, which He ignores. Even worse, the prophet is viewed by the people as nothing more than "one who sings love songs with a beautiful voice and plays an instrument well" (33:32). Ouch!

Every culture idolizes great singers and highly skilled instrumentalists. Perhaps that's because we watch them doing what we wish we could do. Every time I have recorded in Nashville, surrounded by some of the most accomplished players in the music business, I see firsthand how much I don't know! As I watch and hear these studio musicians transform my songs into smooth guitar patterns or hot licks I always think, *Man I wish I could do that!* Similarly, American television viewers have been inundated with shows like *American*

Idol, America's Got Talent, and most recently *The Voice.* Viewers spend hours watching these programs, seeking the next big vocal star to admire or emulate. And yet God makes it clear to Ezekiel that there is a level of high musical excellence through passionate singing and skilled instrumentation—in the context of worship—that means nothing to Him. When this kind of great musical offering is given to God, it finds its value through congregants who not only hear the sermons and the teachings, but who put those principles into practice. When there is a lack of integration between the musical presentation in worship and the behavior of the worshipper, the music becomes "nothing more than one who sings love songs with a beautiful voice" (Ezek. 33:32) in the ears of God. In other words, we are trivial at best. Apparently God isn't interested in the best. He is more interested in the sincere.

James, the earthly brother of Jesus, talks of this same principle in his epistle. "Therefore . . . in humility receive the word implanted, which is able to save your souls. But prove yourselves doers of the word, and not merely hearers who delude themselves" (1:21–22, NASB). This is the heart of what God is saying to Ezekiel. When the people who call themselves the people of God simply hear teaching that never translates into behavior, they are deceiving themselves. When we believe that what we offer up in worship is judged by God on the basis of its artistic quality, the passage in Ezekiel 33 reminds us that our assessment is inaccurate. This idea is not only counter to our logic and values but even deceiving to humankind. We hear quality, experience its emotion, and—because what we produce is pleasing to our ears—we naturally assume God must be pleased. Big mistake.

James continues, "For if anyone is a hearer of the word and not a doer, he is like a man who looks at his natural face in a mirror; for once he has looked at himself and gone away, he has immediately forgotten what kind of person he was" (4:23–24, NASB) When the lives of the worshippers do not exemplify the teachings of the God they worship—or the lyrical sentiment of the songs they sing—their music no longer serves as an avenue for worship but a distraction from it. Even if presented with passion and excellence, the music falls on the deaf ears of a God bored by the sounds of people who simply don't get the bigger picture. They sing and make music in celebration or solemnity, but it is empty and meaningless for the One to which it is directed. It is wallpaper worship.

RULES, RULES, AND MORE RULES

Isaiah, another Old Testament prophet, gives a word from God that rings consistent with the words of Amos and Ezekiel: "This people draw near with their mouth / and honor me with their lips, / while their hearts are far from me, / and their fear of me is a commandment taught by men" (29:13).

Martin Luther's Protestant Reformation was indeed a reaction to the church's practice of establishing man-made rules over biblical principles. The church's mission and identity was so overshadowed by traditions and laws made up by church leaders and wealthy nobles that for centuries those laws drained the church, and its people, of spirit and life. Luther's "Ninety-five Theses" were a direct challenge to those church laws, showing them to be arbitrary rules of men rather than biblical mandates of God. When Luther published a New Testament in his native German language, the people began to read for themselves what was important to God. The people's own reaction to the church's overreach was felt all over Europe and eventually the world. Luther's revolt not only formed the Protestant church but also changed government, art, music, architecture, and literature; and started wars that lasted for generations. Yet, for the first time, worshippers saw themselves as royal priests (see 1 Pet. 2:9) who could not only read and interpret the Bible for themselves but could also sing together their praises as a result. Again, once worshippers were shown the truth, they could easily spot what was false.

German hymnody was born from the Reformation. Hymns such as "Praise to the Lord, the Almighty" and many others were direct expressions of the joy of reformed Christians set free from over one thousand years of church oppression. "A Mighty Fortress Is Our God" became the anthem of the Reformation. It is still in use today in mainstream Protestant music repertoire. Songwriter Tommy Walker arranged an excellent rock anthem version of the hymn, which was used in the Promise Keepers events in 1996–1998.

This is the essence of what Jesus was communicating to the woman at the well of Sychar in John 4. She said to Him, "Our people say we should worship at this mountain, but you Jews say people should worship in Jerusalem. Which is it?" His answer is consistent with Isaiah, Ezekiel, and Amos: It is none of the above. God is looking for something *within* our worship which goes way beyond the rules.

TRUE WORSHIP: AN EYE PUZZLE

Eye puzzles are popular. It's fun to look at these images and see one thing when someone next to you is looking at the same image but sees something completely different. Once the hidden image is recognized, it is the only thing you see when you look at it again.

True worship is like that. Once you have experienced worship that is powerful, participatory, and pleasing to God, you are much more likely to recognize it when it happens and much more likely to sense when it is not happening. Once we experience what is true, the false is easy to spot.

Musicians are quick to equate worship with the music they personally produce. We are a proud bunch! So of course the religious music we compose glorifies God and calls down His presence when listened to or sung by people. How dare anyone suggest otherwise? Meanwhile, some of the longest lasting and most widely recognized religious music was composed by people who were not adherents to religious norms or even what we would consider a Christian lifestyle.

In the 1984 movie *Amadeus*, a fictional movie based on the music and life of composer Wolfgang Amadeus Mozart, the competing and sinister composer named Salieri is enraptured with the form, emotion, and content of Mozart's compositions. In his self-righteous arrogance, Salieri asks, "Why would God choose an obscene child to be His instrument?"[1] When you get to know musicians personally, you find most of us to be obscene children. Ask my wife—or just go on an extended road tour with musicians.

When God's presence and power seem elusive or absent from our forms of worship—musical or otherwise—we can make the mistake of rationalizing that our forms of worship *are* worship, when actually our forms of worship are simply *forms* of worship, not worship itself. It is natural to synonymize our forms of worship with worship itself. It is especially understandable when you realize that the job of composing songs used for worship is a huge publishing business, generating millions of dollars in royalties from public church use and radio airplay. Could there possibly be a conflict of interest? Don't kid yourself. Of course there could be. However, be careful to judge wisely with this issue. The revenues generated by the song publishing industry are neutral. They can be used for good, to sustain and provide for a creative process that is worthy. But to not recognize the other option is denial. The basic business model can become a conflict of interest when the publishing company's schedule demands new material to be put into the church marketplace. This market-driven fact begs the question: Is the plethora of new songs being released the result of the writers' experiences of God's presence and power in their lives and communities? Or are they being written and released because of publishing deadlines? The answer could be that both are true. But the anonymous public user of those songs doesn't know and can't know. We are simply accepting the repertoire as "the latest songs we are expected to use in the service of worship." Rather than blindly accepting everything that's put out into what is now a commercial "worship market," I have found that separating the concepts of music and worship is not only healthy, it is a method of accountability.

DOES MUSIC EVER BECOME WORSHIP?

Many believers have experienced times when the corporate expression through song was so heartfelt and powerful, they were transcended into something beyond the moment. As a leader, there have been times when I would simply back off from the microphone and let the people hear themselves leading themselves. If you are a musical worship leader, try this. Ask the musicians to stop playing and the other singers to stop singing. Let your people sing their praise to God together, unencumbered, free from the reins of human leadership. (Logically, this can happen only if the congregation knows the song.) If they sing without the leader's vocals, paying no attention to whomever is on the platform but engaged vertically in unity with each other—not with the song or the music but in spiritual expression to the unseen Spirit of God—it is a sign the leaders have actually led. Like sheep with a shepherd, the flock has been led to the pure water, and they're doing what they came to do—they are drinking it.

This is when music becomes worship. And when it happens, everyone knows it. There is a presence of God's Spirit that is powerful, convicting, unifying, undeniable, and yet unseen. It makes all the times when we crank out music in a worship context seem like a training exercise to hopefully, eventually experience a moment such as this. When a congregation experiences this kind of worship, they know it is something extraordinary. They will also look with anticipation for when, or if, it happens again. They will quickly recognize when this is not happening as well.

What is God seeing, hearing, and receiving in our corporate worship week to week? Is what we are producing in church a true corporate expression of sincere hearts turned toward God? Are the people participating? Are they singing? Are they engaged? Are they practicing what they are singing in the lyrics or hearing in the sermon when they are in traffic, at work, at home, in their relationships, or is it simply what Isaiah called "lip service?" Are we equating the deep acts of worship with the music or forms we are producing?

Worship and music are two separate entities. We need to leave behind our cultural way of speaking and thinking and align ourselves with what the Bible teaches us on this matter. We need to stop assuming that because we are doing music in a worship setting that our music is worship. Our music isn't any more equal to worship than a wafer and cup of juice become the literal and actual body and blood of Christ because of ancient ritual verbiage. Music isn't any more equivalent to worship than baptism is equivalent to salvation. Equating music with worship does not make that music worship. When we do equate music and worship, it is easy to fall into wallpaper worship.

PART THREE:

WHAT WORSHIP CAN BE

9

THREE THINGS MISSED IN TRADITIONAL WORSHIP

Tradition is the living faith of the dead, traditionalism is the dead faith of the living.

—Jaroslav Pelikan

My dad chose to become a military chaplain after he graduated from seminary and pastored a number of churches. His decision to join the air force chaplaincy was one he never regretted. It was a decision my siblings and I never regretted either. Here's why.

Since his tours of duty rotated every three years, we grew up in various places across the United States. We also spent three years in Germany. During our Germany years, we traveled throughout Europe, seeing sites, museums, and cathedrals—everything from the heart of Reformation Germany to Mars Hill in Athens and Vatican City in Rome. By the time I was in seventh grade, we had moved back to the United States and I was attending a public school near the air force base in

Oklahoma where we were stationed. To my civilian classmates, these places were just places in a history book. To me, they were very real.

But beyond the benefits of geography, Dad also served alongside chaplains from various denominational and clerical backgrounds. At each installation, there were chaplains who were Methodists, Lutherans, Episcopalians, Presbyterians, Pentecostals, and Catholic priests. This unique multidenominational ministry within the military exposed me to how a broad spectrum of Christians worshipped. As my childhood was playing out in the pews of air force chapels, a lot of change was taking place in the cultural, as well as worship, fabric of America. While the military community was caught up in Vietnam War deployments and casualties, the cultural unrest of our nation was exploding.

> The 1960s began with the election of John Kennedy, the first president born in the twentieth century. For many Americans, the young president was the symbol of a spirit of hope for the nation. When Kennedy was murdered in 1963, many felt that their hopes died, too. This was especially true of young people, and members and supporters of minority groups.

> A time of innocence and hope soon began to look like a time of anger and violence. More Americans protested to demand an end to the unfair treatment of black citizens. More protested to demand an end to the war in Vietnam. And more protested to demand full equality for women.

By the middle of the 1960s, it had become almost impossible for President Lyndon Johnson to leave the White House without facing protesters against the war in Vietnam. In March of 1968, he announced that he would not run for another term.

In addition to President John Kennedy, two other influential leaders were murdered during the 1960s. Civil rights leader Martin Luther King Junior was shot in Memphis, Tennessee in 1968. Several weeks later, Robert Kennedy—John Kennedy's brother—was shot in Los Angeles, California. He was campaigning to win his party's nomination for president. Their deaths resulted in riots in cities across the country.

The unrest and violence affected many young Americans. The effect seemed especially bad because of the time in which they had grown up. By the middle 1950s, most of their parents had jobs that paid well. They expressed satisfaction with their lives. They taught their children what were called "middle class" values. These included a belief in God, hard work, and service to their country.

Later, many young Americans began to question these beliefs. They felt that their parents' values were not enough to help them deal with the social and racial difficulties of the 1960s. They rebelled by letting their hair grow long and by wearing strange clothes. Their dissatisfaction was strongly expressed in music.[1]

In the middle of this social unrest and cultural change, the Christian church was experiencing change as well. By 1965, The Catholic Church Council known as Vatican II gave approval to the "folk mass," introducing guitars and informality into the Catholic liturgy. On the heels of Vatican II came the Jesus movement (1968–1972), changing the way the Protestant church worshipped from the outside in. Guitars, drums, and folk/rock instruments began to creep into mainstream denominational worship sanctuaries. Even in our military chapels, change was in the air.

Attending worship services at a military chapel was quite different from what my civilian churchgoing counterparts experienced. Most civilian churches had one head pastor. In the military chapel, each worship service would take on the denominational style of whichever Protestant chaplain was "on duty" each week. In a Lutheran-led service, I remember reading through what seemed like long liturgical sections, while the sermon portion was only ten minutes long. Presbyterians, I noticed, liked to sing Scottish hymns and would occasionally sprinkle a baby with baptismal water. The Episcopalians were like Lutherans on steroids, and the Methodists seemed to me like a balance between Baptist and Presbyterian. My dad's Baptist-styled services were fairly informal compared to the others: a few hymns, Scripture reading, offertory, and a long sermon. Sometimes he'd go out on a limb and give an "invitation" (a Baptist term for inviting people to come forward during the final song to become a Christian or, in civilian settings, to also become a member of the local church).

As a youngster, I wondered about the meaning of certain elements within the services and how they got there. I remember many of the worship services feeling stiff, the result of the traditional style as well as the formality of the military culture. But I also remember many meaningful moments. The old air force hymn, "Lord, Guard and Guide the Men Who Fly," would close many of those worship services, and its lyrics still affect me to this day.[2] I still run into military retirees who remember the impact my dad's preaching had on their lives. Even with its military formality, there were times when it seemed the congregation "got it."

WHAT IS "TRADITIONAL" WORSHIP?

Before we go forward, let me specify what I mean by a traditional service. Most that I have attended are actually not very traditional. With a few exceptions, the only difference between most traditional and contemporary services seems to be the choice of musical style and the level of informality. So for the sake of this comparison, I will be referring to traditional worship services as those that include:

- Some lighter liturgical elements such as creeds and written prayers (e.g., the Lord's Prayer, prayers of confession and absolution, responsive readings)
- Corporate practice of sacraments, such as baptism and Communion
- Traditional musical elements expressed through various instruments outside of a typical rhythm section, including music that is primarily chosen from the body of church

sacred music—hymns, traditional gospel music, Handel's "Messiah," Bach's "Passions," and later works by legitimate composers (eg., John Ness Beck, Aaron Copland)

Also within our working definition of "traditional" would be full liturgical orders such as Episcopal, Anglican, or Lutheran, which are considered Protestant by theology but, because of liturgies that are driven by the church calendar, would feel more Catholic to an evangelical. So let's think outside the box together as we launch into what I call the "box busters."

EMOTION

Who made the rule that traditional services need to be devoid of human emotion? This mind-set comes from the historical reality that Christian tradition roots are formed from a western Greek orientation. Greeks were rational, linear thinkers. Hebrews, on the other hand, were more emotional, demonstrative, and tactile in their learning.

When we think how Christian worship was to be laid out, we have to go as far back as AD 364 and the Council of Laodicea.[3] The canon rules of worship forbade congregational participation and gave the service over to the hierarchy to perform the rites of worship for the people. When you understand why, it makes sense. In the fourth century, the Roman Empire was at its peak under the reign of Constantine. After almost four hundred years of Christian oppression, Christianity had become the official religion of the empire. Churches, monasteries, and schools were popping up all over Europe. There was a legitimate fear of heretical practices creeping into church worship. The Council felt the need to take control of the worship process that was probably run amuck by uneducated congregants all over Europe.

That said, a lot of years have passed since AD 364. Can we get over it now? What does it take for traditional church leaders to guide their people into a worship experience in spirit and truth while still using ancient elements of worship?

SWEET HOME ALABAMA

I experienced such a church when I was in Montgomery, Alabama, performing and speaking at the Air Force Officer's Basic Course Chapel at Maxwell Air Force Base. During my stay, I was also asked to provide music for a local Episcopal congregation. Even though I agreed to do it, I went with preconceived notions. First, I knew that it would be highly liturgical, meaning all the parts would be read by the rector and then the people would respond. As in the Catholic tradition, from which Episcopalians get their roots, the climax of the service is Communion, the celebration of the Eucharist. This is why they build their sanctuaries with the Communion altar in the center of the platform surrounded by kneeling rails, where congregants come forward and kneel to receive the elements. You also see two lecterns up front: one to the right and one to the left, as opposed to just one large pulpit that is front and center like in Baptist, Pentecostal, or gospel traditions.

My job that Sunday was to provide music during the Communion portion of the service while congregants filed up to the front, kneeled at the railing, and ate the elements of the Eucharist. Since this moment happens at the end of the service, there are a lot of readings and responses to go through to get there. I had been through all of this before and was ready for the drill. But this church's approach to the liturgy was different than what I had experienced. The leaders read their parts with articulation, energy, and thoughtfulness. The people in turn responded with articulation, energy, and thoughtfulness. There was a back-and-forthness about what was happening that reminded me of some of the traditional African American churches I have attended. Those predominantly white southern Episcopalians were getting it because they were being led by leaders who got it.

After the people somberly prayed a prayer of confession of sin in unison, the rector declared them forgiven because of the blood sacrifice and resurrection of Jesus. He enthusiastically declared, in traditional Episcopal fashion, their absolution from sin. He stated in a loud voice, "You are clean because of the blood of the Lamb of God!" The people responded, "Praise be to God!" And then they broke out in hugs for one another, saying to one another, "Praise be to God!" While they were hugging one another, the rector and his Communion assistant changed out of their liturgical robes and into robes of blood red. They were ready to serve the Eucharist. The people were electric with anticipation.

They signaled for me to come forward. I was to take Communion first at the railing so I could move over to play my guitar and provide the music for this portion of the service. As I knelt there alone, with my hands lifted in surrender, the rector and his assistant administered a wafer to me, placing it on my tongue. He said to me, "This is the body of the Lord Jesus Christ, broken for you." Then the assistant handed a goblet to the rector, who then put it to my mouth. I drank a sip of the red wine and he said, "This is the blood of the Lord Jesus Christ, the blood of the new covenant, shed for the remission of your sins." Then, he took my face in his hands and said to me, "Danny, Jesus has removed your sins forever and you are clean." I completely fell apart. I began to weep with joy at that railing. It took me a few minutes to regain my composure to then play the music I was there to play, while the rest of the people came forward for the same experience.

I have experienced similar Episcopal and Anglican services in Connecticut, Tennessee, Colorado, Italy, and Korea. For the most part, as a kid in traditional settings, I didn't see pastors, chaplains, or priests leading their people through traditional elements of worship in a way that communicated anything close to what was being recited from up front by the leader. That is a shame. In liturgical worship, lack of emotion misses the original intent of the writers of the liturgy. Reciting liturgical phrases without emotion misses the incredible theology, color, language, and imagery. It's like telling your children a bedtime story in monotone and wondering why they fell asleep.

In her book *Walking On Water*, Madeleine L'Engle writes, "We are afraid of that which we cannot control; so we continue to draw in the boundaries around us, to limit ourselves to what we can know and understand. Thus we lose our human calling because we do not dare to be creators, co-creators with God."[4] The Council of Laodicea's need to control content and participation had reasons of its own, unique to their set of challenges during the fourth century and beyond. But is there something awry when church leadership feels the need to control or stifle a congregation's response to the mystery and majesty of the gospel?

Would we be embarrassed as Simon the Pharisee was (see Luke 7:36–50) if a dishonorable woman threw herself at the mercy of God in our worship service? What are we afraid may happen? When people really understand what the gospel can mean for their families, marriages, careers, and their very lives, should they not be allowed to express it—and even encouraged that it is actually appropriate to express it? I miss emotion in traditional worship.

EXPLANATION

Under the colored light of Sunday morning sun shining through stained glass windows depicting great American war victories, I would sit Sunday after Sunday as a youngster. Sometimes a robed Methodist chaplain would lead the morning Scripture reading. He would read an Old Testament passage, which I usually tuned out—for two reasons:

1. An Old Testament reading was usually something historical, which made no sense to me since it was usually a few verses read without having knowledge of the context.
2. I always thought if it was *Old* Testament it couldn't be useful for much anyway. Wasn't that the point of naming the New Testament the *new* one? I have encountered many adults who have been in church most of their lives, who share the sentiment and the same ignorance.

Following the Old Testament reading, the chaplain would have everyone stand for the New Testament reading. (This practice of standing reinforced my notion that the Old

Testament could not be all that important.) After the New Testament reading, the Methodist chaplain would face the altar with his back to the congregation, the organist would hit a cadence, and we would all sing the "Gloria Patri."[5] The what?! Why are we doing this? Why is he facing away from us? What's going on?

Many well-intentioned traditionalists seem to share a common assumption. They think everyone sitting in the pew knows what they are doing, why they are doing it, and what it means. Maybe that was true in 1951 when people didn't move geographically as much as they do today, and families and communities were somewhat more unified through church life and confirmation classes. Today, assuming that anyone sitting in a church pew should understand the what, why, and how of a traditional service is not only a bad assumption but also a surefire way to bore and run off potential worshippers. Those who don't "get it" feel like outsiders. They may attend once, but they likely may never return.

In many mainline Protestant traditions, it used to be the practice to dedicate the babies and get them into confirmation class as soon as they could learn. By age twelve, they could recite key Scripture verses and identify the founding fathers of the denomination. Certain unique elements of the worship service were explained so that when the liturgist stood at the reading of the New Testament passage with the "Gloria Patri" sung in response, congregants had a clue of what was going on and why.

The problem with this old system is that these mainstream denominations have been losing members for decades. The Religious Landscape Study conducted by Pew Research

Center in 2014 found that 14.7 percent of US adults are affiliated with the mainline Protestant tradition, a sharp decline from 18.1 percent when the last Religious Landscape Study was conducted in 2007. Mainline Protestants have declined at a faster rate than any other major Christian group, including Catholics and evangelical Protestants; and, as a result, that sect is shrinking as a share of all Protestants and Christians.[6]

Some churches don't follow their own denominational guidelines anymore. Instead of denominational and faith history, children's classes consist of everything from Disney movies to Veggie Tales to comic books about a few of the major Bible stories. Kids are dismissed to children's church, so they no longer grow up worshipping with their parents. When they reach middle school and high school, they are rockin' out in the basement, separated from "adult church" until they reach college age. By eighteen, they are ignorant of worship traditions, raised to be separated from adult worship; and because of job or college class schedules, they tank church altogether. The day of confirmation classes as the standard for connecting youth with the traditions of their worship heritage is long gone. So what's the answer?

If worshippers in traditional churches are going to understand the whys and hows of their style of worship, leaders will have to educate congregants as they go. Explanation of the context of certain worship elements to a congregation, as part of the worship service itself, produces a participating congregation.

So what does explanation look like? It's very simple. In the above example of the Scripture reading, the leader takes a moment to explain (a) why we read Scripture; (b) why we will stand during the reading the of New Testament passage, where that tradition began, and why; and (c) what it means to sing in response to the reading itself, what the Latin "Gloria Patri" means, and how it was passed down. It can take all of one minute. Should explanation be done every week? Not necessarily. But feeding the congregation a little at a time can be done with enthusiasm, articulation, planning, and excellence. If it is done right, it can yield the benefits of participation from worshippers who will understand why they are doing what they are doing.

Let's pretend, for example, we are worshipping in a traditional service where, during the New Testament Gospel reading it is customary to stand. Right before the Gospel reading is introduced, the leader could say: "Before we proceed into our Gospel reading, let me take a moment to explain why we stand." Then the leader says: "All of the Bible is God's revealed Word to us. Our ancestors of the faith liked to stand during the Gospel readings as a way of recognizing that it was in the four Gospels—Matthew, Mark, Luke, and John—that the story of Jesus is told. Jesus stood the day He read from the prophet Isaiah in Luke 4:16–20 in the synagogue. Let's do the same, as we read today's passage from the Gospel." This is only one example of what could be shared with a congregation. When Ezra read the law to the people of Israel, they all stood as he read (see Neh. 8:5). Standing represents respect. Standing also represents a posture of attention, the posture of a soldier taking orders from the commander. Any of these ideas can be communicated briefly and succinctly, all for the purpose of inviting the congregants to not only participate, but to understand why they are participating. It can create a unifying moment of an otherwise mundane custom. The same kind of explanation can be done with creeds, Communion, or any other traditional part of a service. Since most ancient segments of worship are out of the ordinary, different from the day-to-day activity of a worshipper's week, or just plain weird, explanation can yield some great rewards. I miss explanation in traditional worship.

EXPECTATION

Who also made the rule that if there are traditional elements of worship, it automatically means that the Holy Spirit cannot be leading the experience? I once heard someone quip, "Pentecostals call it moving with the Spirit. Baptists call it unorganized."

Since traditional services tend to repeat similar elements of style and content, services can become predictable and there is danger in losing the meaning. How is this solved? How can there be spiritual expectation in a liturgical service when it is so planned out and even repetitive?

Following basic elements of the church calendar (Advent, Christmas, Epiphany, Lent, Holy Week, Easter, Pentecost) is a fabulous tool for creating a sense of expectation. Traditional churches have a great opportunity to move their people through a journey of spiritual events throughout the seasons of the year. Congregants can easily be led with traditional elements into a sense of expectation of how God will uniquely speak and reveal Himself through ancient forms that are far more colorful and creative than simply a few songs and a talk. Evangelist Oral Roberts used to say, "Expect a miracle!" And miracles happened in his ministry. Prayers were answered, sicknesses healed, and provision appeared where there was lack.

Can those kinds of things happen as a result of a traditional worship experience? Well, what are we expecting from God when we worship in spirit and in truth? Can God move like that through traditional and even ancient elements of worship? How big is your God? How educated are your congregants? How willing are your leaders?

UNDERSTANDING CREATES EXPECTATION

In Matthew 8:5–13, a Roman centurion approached Jesus in desperation and asked Him to heal his servant who was deathly sick. When Jesus asked the centurion to lead Him to the servant so He could lay His hands on him and heal him, the centurion said to Jesus, "I am a man under authority. I say to this soldier 'do this' and he does it. I know if you just say the word my servant will be healed." Jesus was so impressed with this soldier's understanding of Jesus' authority—and his expectation of that authority—that not only was the servant healed by Jesus' word, but Jesus made a point to say, "I've never seen such great faith in all Israel."

Expecting that something wonderful will take place when we gather to worship the "God of the universe" seems logical. But repetition through forms, whether traditional or otherwise, can drain faith, and without faith Jesus Himself could not perform miracles, even in His hometown of Nazareth. Jesus' promise, "for where two or three are gathered in my name, there am I among them" was not exclusive to nonliturgical styles of worship. The Episcopal congregants in Alabama proved His presence is not only promised but also expected when they gather around their liturgy. They expected no less.

If you attend a traditional church that is boring and repetitious, and there is no expectation of anything out of the ordinary, it may be time to find a church that uses its ancient traditional forms (creeds, liturgy, hymns, Communion) to emotionally and spiritually connect congregants with the God of power and faith. Helen Keller, the first deaf and blind person to earn a bachelor of arts degree, was quoted, "The only thing worse than being blind is having sight but no vision." Leaders who possess such a wide color palette of traditional worship forms, but bore their congregants with those forms, do not lack faith necessarily, but rather vision in how to communicate that faith. Jaroslav Pelikan, a Lutheran theologian and author said, "Tradition is the living faith of the dead; traditionalism is the dead faith of the living. . . . it is traditionalism that gives tradition such a bad name."[7] As worshippers of the Most High God, we can experience traditional worship that is powerful and alive in its expectation that God's presence will be in whatever rituals we practice. Anything else is reminiscent of the high priest Zechariah in Luke 1:5–23 (see chapter 3). Worshipping without expecting God's presence to be felt, sensed, and experienced is wallpaper worship.

Expectation is a feeling that His presence is a Presence with which to be reckoned. Expectation means we are a part of something much greater than our ancient rituals themselves. Expectation is what grows traditional congregations. I miss expectation in traditional worship.

Traditional congregations who "get it" are out there. Unfortunately they are rare, but they don't have to be. When leaders of traditional services season their liturgy with emotion, explanation, and expectation, it can transform dead ritual into living organic worship. Worship that is dead is wallpaper worship. I for one have experienced both and prefer what is alive. How about you?

10

THREE THINGS MISSED IN CONTEMPORARY WORSHIP

There never was a time, I believe, when the reading public was
so large, or so helplessly exposed to the influences of its own time
. . . so shut off from the past.

—T.S. Eliot

I have mentioned the Jesus movement of the late 1960s and early 1970s—how it began in California with drug-drenched hippies discovering this Jesus-character who hung out with prostitutes, tax collectors, and addicts. Was this the same Jesus spoken of in boring mainstream churches of the same '60s and '70s hip era? How could it be? To these young hippies, mainstream traditional churches seemed irrelevant and judgmental. Something fresh and real was born on the beaches of California in the late 1960s; and by 1972, it had swept the country. Young people lined up to be baptized in the ocean to commemorate their newfound lives as Christians—or, as they became known on the streets, Jesus freaks.

These new Christians looked, talked, and dressed nothing like traditional churchgoers. They brought with them their informal dress, their tell-it-like-it-is language, and of course, their music. I remember hearing stories from Jesus freaks who said, "Well, if we are now followers of Jesus, I guess we need to go to church." They would stroll into a stained-glass-windowed church dressed in jeans, T-shirts, and sandals (or barefoot), toting their guitars and sitting on the floor in front of the pews right in front of the platform. Repulsed by these young people's appearance, church ushers dressed in suits and ties would escort them out of the building. Confused and dismayed, the Jesus freaks decided to gather elsewhere with people who looked, talked, and sounded like them. And gather they did. By the thousands. Many of those early gatherings grew and eventually became known as Calvary Chapel, Church On The Way, Melodyland Christian Center, and the Vineyard, and they grew in numbers mainstream traditional churches could only dream of.

The Jesus movement brought change that is still evident today, namely the phenomenon referred to as contemporary Christian music (CCM). By the late 1980s, CCM morphed into what we now know as contemporary praise and worship music. Pastor Tom Stipe of Calvary Chapel Denver once said, "Rock and roll is the new traditional music of the church." In many cases, what became contemporary in style—not simply music but the informality of dress, presentation, and nomenclature—was the wave of a new culture and a reaction to an existing religious culture that sounded like organs, pianos, and choirs, and looked like people who worked in downtown office buildings. As Bob Dylan sang in 1964, "The times they are a-changin.'"[1] And change they did.

As a teenager during the Jesus movement, I can say there are many elements of what became known as contemporary worship that are still very appealing. Having spoken and led music in contemporary worship settings with anywhere from seven to seventy thousand attendees, I have also come to the conclusion that style of worship or musical selection has little to do with whether worship is actually taking place. While I have been bored and annoyed in traditional worship services, I can honestly say some of the most monotone and predictable services I have been involved in have come from the contemporary side of the worship spectrum. Could it be that even in a loud, rocking, casual, concert-like, fog-and-light-filled auditorium, complete with religious-oriented songs and hipster preachers with tattoos, that "worship in spirit and truth" is lost? In other words, it really doesn't matter what a corpse is wearing when the coffin is closed. What's dead is dead no matter how well you dress it up. Here are three things I miss in contemporary worship.

AWE

T-shirt theology says much about our religious culture. One of my favorites was worn by a kid in my youth group: "Jesus is my homeboy." More recently, I saw one that read "Calvinism: #somelivesmatter." Because of our American informalities, the concept of awe in worship may elicit an initial reaction of fear—fear that we are trying to become formal, something we aren't. It may be tough for us to understand the concept of awe in our twenty-first-century mind-set, but let's give it a try.

One doesn't have to travel to Europe to see the architecture of great cathedrals. We have many here in the United States.

The National Cathedral in Washington DC is quite a sight to see. So is Trinity Church near Wall Street in New York City (Alexander Hamilton is buried in the church's yard). In my fair city of Denver, the Basilica of Immaculate Conception is a tourist site. Even in the remote western farmlands of Kansas, the Cathedral of the Plains was built over a seventy-year period by the German immigrants who settled there. They missed their churches from the old country so they decided to build one that felt like home to them. The altar was shipped from Germany and brought to Kansas by railroad and wagon. But whether in Europe or America, the common denominator in all these buildings is that they are built in the gothic style with ceilings that reach over one hundred feet high. Why would people go to so much trouble to build an edifice that high and that detailed?

When I toured the Vatican, the resident historians told us that the purpose of church architecture of this type was so that when people walked into the building they would be captured with a sense of awe—not only for the detail and artistic acumen of those who designed them but also with an awe of God Himself. Congregants would look up, high into the ceiling, and feel that God is higher than the earth, that His presence should elicit a sense of respect and awe. Perhaps this architectural philosophy found its roots in Isaiah 55:9: "For as the heavens are higher than the earth, / so are my ways higher than your ways / and my thoughts than your thoughts." "Revelation Song" captures this grandiose idea of the awe of God: "Filled with wonder, awestruck wonder at the mention of Your name."[2]

As much as I enjoy contemporary worship in converted bowling alleys or Safeway stores, something is lost in a building that seems as common as an everyday office setting. Or in a new structure that looks, feels, and sounds like an everyday version of the live theater venues downtown. Obviously, it's not just about architecture. There is a casualness about contemporary church that should cause us to pause and think. Is this God we worship being given the proper place of dignity in our contemporary corporate expression? Or do we talk and sing about Him like He is our equal, our "homeboy"? Do we give enough place to celebrating the awesome and mysterious wonder of His divinity? In the elements of what we consider contemporary worship, what causes us to be awestruck?

On the other hand, awe can happen in the most casual of settings. Think about sixty thousand men in shorts, T-shirts, and sneakers, trotting into an NFL stadium with no supervision from their wives, moms, or otherwise at the Promise Keepers events I helped produce and direct in the mid-1990s. Before the events started, guys hit beach balls up and down the seating sections, each man signing his name and hometown before randomly volleying it to the next row. Paper airplanes flew, spit wads shot out through drink straws, you name it. It was what happens when guys get together! Yet once the meetings commenced, there would inevitably be moments of sheer awe. It wasn't the men. It wasn't the NFL stadium. It was something indefinable and yet undeniable. It was the presence of God's Spirit. Sometimes He came during moments of silence, which honestly were not often with that much testosterone present.

But there were times in each event when it was evident that a presence greater than our numbers was in our midst. Men would cry openly, stand silently, or break into song not planned by the music team on the stage. In many locations, the attendees would respond to a speaker's message with deafening shouting. Awe. And it had nothing to do with architecture or location. More recently, the Jesus Culture events held around the world experience the same sense of God's awesome presence in hockey and basketball arenas. As much as I miss the awe that is elicited in ancient church architecture or lofty liturgy, awe of God's presence has little to do with buildings, recitations, and man-made art pieces.

When our kids were attending Colorado State University, they invited us to a gathering of Christian students called ONE. It is a worship event that happens once a year when all of the parachurch campus ministries come together to host a student-led worship service. Of course, it was contemporary in style and it was held in a large lecture hall, complete with all the contemporary elements of songs, instruments, amps, sound, and video. The format was simple. They would sing three to four songs in a row followed by someone reading a Scripture, saying a brief word about it, and then asking attendees to break into groups of four to six to pray together—based on the Scripture and whatever that Scripture brought forth for prayer. After a time, the music would gently start again and the same format would follow: three to four songs, a leader with a Scripture, and groups in prayer. This went on for over three hours. But what struck Angela and I was a sense of the awe of God in that hall. God seemed big, in control of the event; and He seemed to be doing awesome things as these students prayed and sang and worshipped Him. There was a sense of anticipation and expectation about what was going on. God's Spirit was given room to work and to move—in power, in volume, in silence. Awe filled the lecture hall.

When the lights flash, the smoke appears, the colors morph, the set changes are flown from the ceiling while the congregants have eyes closed for prayer, and the music is so pristine it elicits passive observance instead of participation, we should ask ourselves: Are *we* impressive or is *God* impressive? We tend to give great credence to human elements of the performing arts, as wonderful as they can be. But the passage in Amos tells clearly how unimpressed God is with our abilities to pull off great art in His name: "Take away from me the noise of your songs; / to the melody of your harps I will not listen. / But let justice roll down like waters, / and righteousness like an ever-flowing stream" (Amos 5:23–24).

From someone who has been a part of some of the largest, most expensive Christian events of our time—as well as leading thirty soldiers in a makeshift chapel in a tent, somewhere in the jungles of South America—I can attest that the times I have experienced the awe of God have never been subject to levels of production.

Why do we continue to do the same things, hoping for a different outcome? Why do we produce contemporary services as if they are a TV show, where a moment of ambiguity may destroy the flow or pace? Is there a moment dedicated to simply reflecting on what was sung or heard or proclaimed? Or are we afraid of quiet? Do congregants need their worship experience to be similar to what they are experiencing on YouTube, streaming video, or reality TV?

ANAMNESIS

Anamnesis is the opposite of amnesia. Instead of the state of forgetting, anamnesis is the state of remembering. Why is contemporary worship so ahistorical? Who made the rule that anything historic or ancient is not allowed in contemporary worship settings? When I have made this suggestion to some leaders or pastors, I have been met with the reaction that I am exhibiting a complete disconnect with popular trends. Am I?

Recently, our daughters, Corina and Alisha, invited us to attend services where they worship. It is a church-plant meeting in a high school auditorium in downtown Colorado Springs. The setting was typical, the music was the usual, the format was predictable. Until something completely out of the ordinary happened! The pastor said, "Now it's time for the Nicene Creed." The crowd cheered! The pastor gave explanation to the Nicene Creed's origins and its purpose. Then he gave instruction: "When we read it on the screens together, and a particular phrase resonates with your experience in Christ or perhaps your journey of faith this week, give a shout out." And shout out they did. The Nicene Creed was read aloud in unison and the congregants cheered as they read. Digging into it, they read things like this:

The third day He rose again, according to the Scriptures; and ascended into heaven, and sits on the right hand of the Father.

And this:

And He shall come again, with glory, to judge the quick and the dead; whose kingdom shall have no end.

And how about this for an ending?

And I believe one holy catholic and apostolic Church. I

acknowledge one baptism for the remission of sins; and I look for the resurrection of the dead, and the life of the world to come. Amen.[3]

The place came unglued. Who wouldn't want to cheer? This pastor was leading his people to worship with an ancient creed. That is anamnesis.

I shared this story with a friend of mine who grew up Catholic. Before I could finish telling him how this church recited the creed, he interrupted me: "Oh my, I'll bet that was painful for the people." Painful? Maybe that was his experience as a kid growing up in a wallpaper worship liturgical church. But this church? The recitation of the ancient creed was fulfilling, exciting, and relevant to the faith of this congregation; and it was so informal, spontaneous, and fresh. How interesting that we can become so closed to using ancient elements in a contemporary setting because our own exposure to the use of those elements found them drowning in dead ritual.

Anamnesis is the reason I use old hymns in contemporary settings. My reason relates back to chapter 3, "Worship Is Our Heritage." It is only our heritage if we are aware of our heritage.

I was singing in the army chapel service at Fort Leonard Wood, Missouri on a Sunday morning. Before the service started, the chaplain asked me if I would play something during the passing of the offering plates. I thought to myself that I should maybe do an older song, since all of my stuff was new to the ears of the congregants. So I pulled out "Be Thou My Vision," an old Irish hymn I had loved since childhood. When the service was over a teen male approached me. He had dark makeup over his eyes, rings in his pierced lip and ears, and black dyed hair. He looked like Marilyn Manson. He said, "Dude, that song you sang during the offering about vision. That was an awesome song. Did you write that?" I took a moment to explain to him that "Be Thou My Vision" was from ninth-century Irish Christians. He was blown away. In that moment, he was connected to his worship heritage. Without the explanation, he would have left the service thinking he had heard something new. Anamnesis, the art of remembering, contributed a depth to his experience that morning that otherwise may never have come.

When we bring the old into the new we join arms with the great forerunners of our faith. Those who labored over these creeds and hymn lyrics, who wrote them out of persecution, hardship, death, or peace, left us incredible gifts. These ancient gifts can be used in the service of worship no matter what the culture, style, or location. Worshippers who understand the historic connection experience a deeper sense of belonging to something more than their present generation.

After I finished college, I took a job as a youth pastor at a large church near Oklahoma City. It was known as a cool church—informal, using the contemporary music of the day, a popular place to attend. As Christmas approached, I got the brilliant idea of taking our youth on a Christmas caroling hayride. We would ride in a big hay truck, going around to neighborhoods singing the Christmas carols. Then we'd go back to the church and have hot chocolate! Everyone was excited. We piled in the truck and took off.

When we stopped at the first few houses, we jumped out and I said, "Okay, let's sing 'Joy To The World.'" The kids started: "Joy to the world, the Lord is come! Let earth receive her King . . . let everybody come . . . to church and homenimem . . . and wearing heavens ring, and heaven and nature's thing . . ."

Me: "Okay, so we don't know that one. Let's try 'Silent Night.'"

Kids: "Silent night! Holy night! All is calm, all is bright . . . 'round some virgin, monster, and child . . . heaven and nature singing awhile . . ."

Me: "Okay, so we don't know that either. What do you guys know?"

Kids: "Here comes Santa Claus, here comes Santa Claus, right down Santa Claus Lane . . ." (ad infinitum)

The rest of the secular songs—"Jingle Bells," "Jolly Old Saint Nicholas," "Rockin' Around the Christmas Tree"—went off without a hitch. They knew every lyric. As I went through my first Advent/Christmas season in this job, it became evident why the kids knew no Christmas carols. In all the weeks leading up to Christmas Eve, no Christmas carols were sung in the main services, only the latest contemporary worship songs. Finally, on Christmas Eve, some of the carols were reluctantly pulled out. The adults, many of whom never grew up in church, had failed to pass them on. But guess who did pass something on? The public schools. Since schools banned the singing of religious Christmas carols decades ago, they have successfully passed on all secular holiday and winter songs, leaving any religious references for Christmas in the dust. So the kids are proficient in singing about Santa Claus, but have no repertoire of the Christmas carols which are indigenous to their Christian faith. News flash: Those songs about Christ at Christmas belong to the church. They are not the government's heritage. They are the church's heritage. But if the church won't sing them, who will? If kids from church don't know them, whose kids do? We have inherited a great body of songs, liturgies, poems, prose, and art. When there is no anamnesis there is amnesia. When there is no remembrance, our lives and experience become ahistoric.

In Frank Gaebelein's book *The Christian, the Arts, and Truth*, he quotes what English author and poet T.S. Eliot said of readers of his day: "There never was a time, I believe, when the reading public was so large, or so helplessly exposed to the influences of its own time. There never was a time when those who read, read so many more books by living authors than by dead authors. There never was a time so parochial, so shut off from the past."[4] Have we so deliberately shut ourselves and our congregations off from the past that we have become parochial in our quest to be hip and relevant? A young chaplain once asked me at my workshop, "Is it okay for me to introduce responsive reading of Scripture in my contemporary service since that isn't considered contemporary?" Really?

Is there value in educating while leading congregants into deep spiritual matters using the illustrations of the past in our more informal contemporary style? Could our contemporary church attendees relate to the radical stands Martin Luther took against the church and the government? How about teaching on others who went before us to pave roads of religious freedom in the face of tyranny, like Dietrich Bonhoeffer and other martyrs whose shoulders all western Christians stand on? I miss the art of remembering in the context of our twenty-first-century style—the depth of ancient elements—the language of creeds. Passing on our heritage in worship is not limited to cold cathedrals. I miss anamnesis in contemporary worship.

ATTRIBUTION

We are a literal culture. We like our movies to be realistic. We talk openly about many things other cultures and generations before us considered inappropriate. Personally, I like that about the age in which we live. Our contemporary services tend to reflect this commitment to honesty and literalism. Attribution means to attribute extraordinary meaning to something that is ordinary. It is the exercise of taking something common and making it special. Jesus did this when He took the two elements of the leftover Passover dinner and gave them extraordinary meaning, the bread—His body—and the wine—His blood.

Upon entering the auditorium of a large church we visited, there were baskets containing Communion packets. These are shrink-wrapped plastic packets containing a wafer and a cup of juice. I was familiar with these from being in the field with soldiers. Military chaplains use these Communion tools for the convenience and time saver they are in combat theaters—especially when you have only fifteen minutes in which to conduct a Protestant service which will celebrate Communion among a group of soldiers from diverse denominational backgrounds.

During the large church worship service, I was anticipating being led into the sacrament of Communion as I held the packet in my hands. As the service progressed and we watched the band, heard the announcements, listened to more music, and eventually received the morning sermon, I got tired of holding it, so the packet went on the floor under my theater-styled seat. The service finally came to an end. As we were leaving, we passed the Communion packet basket in the lobby and I remembered I had left mine under the seat. There was no reference in the service to what these packets contained, what the elements represented, how to take them, when to take them, and who should take them. The implication was you can take it in your car or in the bathroom or whenever you want in your seat during whatever time in the service you desire, in between sipping your coffee and munching your doughnut. Attribution is taking the simple and not leaving it simple; but, instead, making it mirror the divine.

If we are asking the question, "Is it contemporary?" instead of "Is it worship?" perhaps we are asking the wrong question. In the previous chapter, I excoriated the lack of explanation in many traditional worship experiences. The same exclusion of "why we do what we do" can be evident in contemporary settings as well. The test is simple: Are we leading our people to an understanding of their heritage, their privilege, and their duty? We may be drawing in the unchurched, but are they leaving our services as unchurched as when they came in? How will congregants know to experience something extraordinary unless we lead them into something extraordinary?

"We don't care about stuff like that," said one leader I talked with. "We just want to rock." Fine. But in a rockin' setting, is there no place for mystery, symbolism, and attribution? Is everything of this gospel so literal? From what I am told around the country, millennials, as well as seasoned believers, desire to be transcended into something larger than the culture they live with the other six days of the week. An editorial by Rachel Held Evans in the *Washington Post* reveals much.

> What finally brought me back, after years of running away, wasn't lattes or skinny jeans; it was the sacraments. Baptism, confession, Communion, preaching the Word, anointing the sick—you know, those strange rituals and traditions Christians have been practicing for the past 2,000 years. The sacraments are what make the church relevant, no matter the culture or era. They don't need to be repackaged or rebranded; they just need to be practiced, offered and explained in the context of a loving, authentic and inclusive community. . . .
>
> One need not be an Episcopalian to practice sacramental Christianity. Even in Christian communities that don't use sacramental language to describe their activities, you see people baptizing sinners, sharing meals, confessing sins and helping one another through difficult times. Those services with big screens and professional bands can offer the sacraments, too.[5]

Millennials I meet with around the country seem to agree. What was started by baby booming Jesus freaks and continued with contemporary Christian music has morphed into a slick package that is effective at some levels but lacks an authenticity that many desire. So yes, let's rock! Let's be our informal selves. Who says we cannot also be those who inject a sense of awe, anamnesis, and attribution into our contemporary worship culture? If we have the guts to try, we may find the wallpaper starting to peel—not from high audio volume and thumping subwoofers, but from the power of simple authenticity.

11

THREE PRINCIPLES OF PLANNING: PARTICIPATION, (UN)PREDICTABILITY, POWER

Plans are worthless, but planning is everything.
—Dwight D. Eisenhower

The Promise Keepers events were sweeping the nation. Anywhere from fifty thousand to seventy thousand men would attend these weekend events to hear speakers challenge them to become men of integrity, men who love their wives like Christ loved the church, men who would participate with other men in their journey of faith, men who would lead lives led by prayer. (Moments from these events can be viewed on YouTube.)

My job as program director was to execute what we called the "minute by minute" (minxmin). It was a spreadsheet detailing every cue for lighting, sound, music selections, video clips, speaker slots, emcee announcements, and segues. When looking through the minxmin, one would think the goal of the weekend was to get through each piece in the program and finish on time. As important as the clock is when you are renting a large venue, the goal of our planning was to treat the minxmin like a menu in a restaurant. Each element was prepared and ready. Each piece had its place. But if the men in the seats were not participating, if the program elements came off as predictable as the sunrise, then what we had planned was exactly what we got—and none of us wanted what we had planned. We wanted God to show up through what we had planned. Our feeling was that anyone could produce a show or a huge pep rally. We wanted something transcendent and were hoping our production, evidenced by our minxmin, would not get in the way of God's presence or power. In some instances, the program did come off exactly as it appeared on the minxmin, but that was the exception. Often, we stood in amazement at how God's Spirit showed up in ways we could have never predicted or produced.

I use three essential keys to guide my planning of a corporate worship event. They are a benchmark for whatever I am planning, no matter the size or demographic of the crowd, the location of the event, or whether I am leading as a speaker or with music. These three keys are participation, (un)predictability, and power.

PARTICIPATION

The hallmark of a leader is simple: People are following a leader. If there is little participation from the people we claim to be leading, it should cause a leader to evaluate *why* the people are not participating. If whatever is happening on the platform is not translating beyond the platform, there is a gap between the platform and the people. We see it all the time in music sections of worship services. Musicians are on the platform, singing their hearts out, playing furiously, seemingly engaged in what they are doing, while the audience is disengaged. (Remember Las Vegas? Reread my preface and introduction.)

In evangelicalism, we hold preaching and speaking as being so central to the communication of the gospel message that if a preacher elicited such a passive response from an audience, I dare say that preacher would be out of a job.[1] As a producer of large Christian events, I've learned that any speaker whose crowd response equated to some sitting, some standing, some sipping coffee, and some talking, that speaker would never be invited back. But for some reason, passivity about music in the worship context is not only tolerated, it is expected. Let's first consider why this happens.

Why? The gap between platform and people is not new in Christian worship, and it was not exclusive to musical presentation. It was happening in the church as early as the medieval ages, prior to the Reformation. (I talked about this earlier, but I am reviewing it for those who skipped it to get to the "practical application" chapters!) People would come to church to watch the priests perform the Mass. The rules of the Mass were stringent. No congregational singing was allowed. The only singing was done by the choristers in a balcony behind the congregation, or in a loft far to the front to the side of the altar. No one except the priest was allowed to approach the altar. Participation was allowed during two of the eight sections of the Mass—the Credo and the Eucharist. The Credo was the congregational recitation of the Nicene Creed as a way to unite believers. The Eucharist (Communion) was accepting the "body and blood of Christ" by orally taking a wafer and being given wine by the priest (congregants did not touch the eucharistic elements). In addition, all of this warm, inviting worship experience was recited in Latin, which was not the native tongue of most of the parishioners. Talk about a gap between platform and people.

We live in the "passive reality show" age. We are all about watching others doing something extraordinary and vicariously living the experience through what we observe. Reality shows, talent contests, and virtual reality have all provided ways to have extraordinary experiences—fake experiences, but experiences we would not have otherwise. Likewise, our worship experience can easily become virtual, an observation other than something in which we are actually involved.[2]

Second, the gap between platform and people exists simply because those on the platform are either unaware of the gap or not concerned by it. Noticing there is distance between the performer (speaker, musician, any role as a platform leader) and the performer's audience is a fundamental observation in any of the performing arts. So why does this gap exist and how do we close it?

USE YOUR BINOCULARS

In the PK stadium events, my station was in a tent to the side of the stage. I was surrounded by video monitors and flanked by my stage manager and administrative assistant. The emcee for the event was always by my side, ready to hear instruction for his next journey onto the stage. I was connected by headset to house sound, stage monitor sound, video truck, our speaker/

artist hospitality team (transporting our guests from airport to hotel to venue to green room to stage and back) and the PK executive leadership team. Activity in that tent could get very truncated and focused on any momentary crisis. However, there was one item in that tent that we used regularly—binoculars. Since the stadiums were so vast, there was no way to walk the aisles in the middle or upper sections to see how the program elements were connecting with the attendees, while staying connected to platform duties. The binoculars served to let us see if what we were doing on the platform was connecting with the men in the seats, even to the upper sections at the top.

This principle of the binoculars is in Proverbs 27:23: "Know well the condition of your flocks." This is the first step in solving the participation problem. We must recognize it, then watch and observe those we are leading. John Cleese, the talented actor and writer for the English comedy troupe Monty Python, commented on the importance of this principle: "If you can't see the faces of the people you're performing comedy for, then you are dead because you cannot adjust what you're doing based on their responses."[3] If a comedian's endgame is laughs and he or she understands this principle of adjustment based on an audience's response, how much more important is it for those who lead congregations in song, speaking, or liturgy?

KNOW YOUR STUFF

A speaker or a musician must know their stuff so well that they can deliver it without thinking about the mechanics of delivery. If I am playing a song or giving a talk, I need to know my material so well that, while I deliver it, I am actually outside of my delivery observing the response from my audience. As I am observing my audience's response, I am thinking about the next piece of my talk or the next song I will perform. If my audience is not connecting with what I am doing, they are telling me "I am not in the mood for this" or "I don't understand what you are telling me." As I observe their quandary, I am already changing what I will do for the next segment of my presentation. All this observation, evaluation, and audible-play-changing is taking place simultaneously while I am delivering my performance. If you are to be an effective leader on the platform, you have to know your stuff so well that you can do it without thinking about the mechanics of doing it. This takes rehearsal and repetition.

Linda Ronstadt was an icon in the 1970s and '80s, selling millions of recordings, winning multiple Grammys, and packing arenas on tour. Later in her career, she left rock to sing "The Great American Songbook," the classic tunes of the 1930s, '40s, and '50s, with the lush orchestrations of the Nelson Riddle Orchestra. In an interview on *Good Morning America*, Linda was asked about her early days starting as a singer: "I would sing in rehearsals for eight hours a day, five to six days a week." She went on to say in the interview how it not only made her voice stronger, wider, and more versatile, but also made performing instinctive.[4]

The instinct to be able to speak, sing, or perform from a platform is not something every preacher, singer, or performer is born with. It takes hours, weeks, and years of discipline and dedication to the craft to be able to deliver instinctively, while reading your audience and making any presentation changes that may be necessary on the spot.

A FAMILIAR VOICE

Music (worship) leaders must lead in a way that audiences find familiar. Those who choose to lead with all new songs will find few followers.[5] Familiarity sends a message that invites people to participate. Recently, I read in a worship blog: "The more they sing with you, the more they will trust you." My experience is the opposite: The more they trust you, the more they will sing with you. When people sense an invitation from the platform to come along, and it is familiar territory, they will follow. If audiences detect an attitude of "we are the pros—just leave this to us," they will not engage because they haven't been invited. This is when wallpaper worship turns congregants into wallflower worshippers. Wallflowers are the people at parties who sit quietly in a chair because no one asks them to dance, and they are too shy to get up and dance by themselves. We have churches full of wallflower worshippers.

Back in chapter 6, I quoted from blogger Don Chapman's article "Why Rock Star Worship Leaders Are Getting Fired." He talks about a friend of his who applied for an open worship leader job at a large church through an employment agency. The agency indicated that there were *many* of these jobs open. The reason?

> As my friend looked at the [song] set list from the past six weeks, he noticed *not a single song was repeated.* . . . They're performing worship songs, not leading them. One big reason my friend's church fired their [worship leader] was that they were concerned their congregation wasn't worshipping

during the music. Of course they weren't—they
didn't know any of the songs![6]

Some of the greatest moments in the PK stadium events
were when the band stopped playing and seventy thousand
men were led to sing one or two verses of "Amazing Grace"
a cappella. The worship leader suddenly becomes "one of us"
rather than a professional musician we are observing from a
distance. Familiarity can bring together the gap between platform and people, and invite a transcendent moment. Participation plummets when there is little trust. Trust is difficult to
achieve without familiarity.

I encourage musicians to introduce no more than one to
three new songs a month. If one doesn't take, ditch it and find
another one that does connect with the congregation. Just because songs are on the most recent playlist on Christian radio
does not mean they will necessarily work for corporate singing.[7]
(I will cover how to choose new songs that will elicit participation in the next chapter.)

Since worship is our heritage, I encourage musicians
to learn historic music. We all realize hymns can be stiff in
structure and old in form. Yet many have deep and meaningful lyrics.[8] The older repertoire also has a history with many
believers. Using hymns can be a challenge to the self-taught
musician, but it can be done. (In the next chapter, we will
explore how to break apart a hymn, make it work for modern
instruments, and how to determine when to leave them alone
or leave them out altogether.) When we use songs from the
historic repertoire, we are passing on the musical part of our
worship heritage.

SIMPLY BECAUSE WE CAN

A pastor cues the band to come back to the platform after the sermon for a final song. He's making a transition while they take their place. Suddenly the fog starts, lights change, sets move, and the sound of automatic digital audience lighting hums. It's as if we have put ourselves into a box: "Let's all sing. But wait! We can't 'worship' until the spots turn blue with fog, the screens switch to the slide with the cloud motif, and the audience spots turn 45 degrees! . . . Okay, we are clear to go. Now let's worship." Why do we do this? Because we can.

When I toured churches, chapels, and even some colleges in the early 1990s, we would haul our own sound system with us because many of the smaller venues I was playing were not updated with professional sound gear.[9] While the 1990s were when PK stadium events were at their apex—and more popular Christian bands were starting to play arenas—sound gear in average churches was less than ideal. Those days are gone, thank God. The church has caught up with technology. The kinds of tools and gear the church uses today were seen in large concert venues, Broadway show theaters, or nightclubs only twenty years ago. For instance, when I flew to Mogadishu, Somalia in 1994 to perform for our combat troops, we flew my sound system with me on a C-5 transport. By 2011, when I toured our forward bases in Iraq and Kuwait, there was a professional sound system in every little makeshift combat chapel. Even when I attended my grandmother's memorial service at her rural church in Louisiana, the platform was full of cables, keyboard rigs, a drum cage, mics, amps, and stage monitors.

The question we need to ask is: "Just because we *can*, should we?" I had a conversation with a leader of a huge church with multiple campuses. I was told that the lighting director of this church was on his knees asking God to show him whether he should use a blue spot or a red spot on the fog during a particular line in a particular song. That kind of dedication to the craft of lighting and prayer is indeed impressive. But really? If the people are simply standing there observing all the glitz, is that the prayer that needs to be prayed? Are we asking the right questions? Are the live music and visual effects we are producing inviting people to participate, or simply listen and observe what we know how to do? Just because we can reproduce live sound and visual effects that a few years ago could only be produced in a studio, our job as leaders of worshippers has not changed.

Use your binoculars. Know the condition of your flock. Adjust what you are doing—song choices, speaking style, your use of techno gear—until you see them engaging with it. Participation plummets when there is an atmosphere that distances the commoners from the priests or the amateurs from the pros. When you see them participating, you know you have earned their trust. When there are followers—only then should one assume the title of "leader."

(UN)PREDICTABILITY

When Angela and I are home from traveling, it is often our routine in the evening to turn on the local news. We have found that we've favored one station over the others through the years. Why? Predictability. We know the personalities of the anchors, what their backdrop and desks look like, and the opening bumper music. When there is a line of eighteen cars going through the McDonald's drive-thru, it is largely because people know what they are going to get. Predictability works well for local news shows and fast food. A weekly worship service, however, is different. While familiarity can bring an audience in, predictability can also drive them away. We need to plan with an eye toward *un*predictability. Here are some considerations for planning a service that is familiar yet unpredictable.

LET JUXTAPOSITION WORK FOR YOU

I have often used this idea in situations where I am invited to lead. When I am in a contemporary culture, I introduce a few traditional elements. When in a traditional setting, I introduce some contemporary elements. This is not arbitrary. It is for the purpose of unpredictability. For instance, if I see that a congregation uses exclusively Christian contemporary or radio airplay selections for their worship music, I will, of course, choose those for familiarity. But I will also introduce something from our heritage: a hymn, a creed, a responsive antiphonal Scripture reading. If it is Advent or Lent, I will talk about the significance of the tradition and introduce a moment of worship around those more traditional elements. The feedback I get is usually one of two responses: "Hmm . . . well, that was different" or, more commonly, "Wow, that was really meaningful" (or "Dude, did you write that?!") Either way, introducing the unpredictable can be a way of leading people to a place they would not go otherwise.

WHAT IS THE END RESULT SUPPOSED TO LOOK LIKE?

With all the planning and elements of a service, is this question being asked? And—even more important—is this question being answered? Without considering the end result, predictability can creep in. Like I said in the introduction, we may have the talent, the gear, and the facilities; but if we aren't getting the ball over the goal line, we aren't winning. This is why Vince Lombardi had his players get back to the basics of the game. But do we even know where the goal line is?

AVOID THE TEMPTATION TO GO TOO CASUAL.

Our casual culture can be warm and inviting. It can also cause us to lose the power and dignity of worship. On many occasions, I have been a part of a service where the leader is so casual in his lead-in that I have had to immediately change how I would follow him. It is important to relate to our audience—to be warm, inviting, and familiar. But avoid the temptation to be so casual that whatever comes afterward is stifled or trivialized.

PAY ATTENTION TO THE ORDER OF PROGRAM ELEMENTS

- Ask yourself, "What comes before or after this element in the program?" For example, after a meaningful song set or a prayer, launching into announcements of upcoming events may not serve the purpose of the moment just created.

- Always ask, "Why are we doing this at this time? Where have we just led our people to? What do they need right now after we have just prayed/sang/received Communion/ fill in your blank?"
- Mix up the order, but only after answering the question "What does the end result look like?" Only then are you free to consider creating an order to your worship service that is new or different. Avoid the temptation to make changes arbitrarily.

A recent trend is to open up for public feedback following a sermon. If it is led well, it can become a tool of explanation (chapter 9) or attribution (chapter 10) within any style of worship. A pastor I knew used to end his sermon and then have a few moments of silent reflection on what was just shared. Questions to ponder appeared on the screen, music softly started, and then a song of participation or devotion/reflection would cap the moment and drive deeply the point of the sermon. (More in the next chapter on moments of declaration, response, and devotion.)

PUBLIC PRAYER—MORE THAN "AUNT TILLY" BACK IN IOWA

Prayer in the corporate context can be very predictable, and unfortunately, it can lead congregants nowhere other than to say they prayed in a worship service. I am finding that younger worshippers want substance over form. Prayer about relevant issues, even specific to congregants, can be a powerful tool to lead participation. Relevance in public prayer can drive the unpredictability in worship.

Ultimately, what we all crave is authenticity. An audience can sense it the moment a leader speaks from a platform. Authenticity can be unpredictable, however. Are we ready for the unpredictable in worship?

POWER

Paul writes to young Timothy, "In the last days there will come times of difficulty. For people will be lovers of self, . . . lovers of pleasure rather than lovers of God, having the appearance of godliness but denying its power. Avoid such people" (2 Tim. 3:1–2, 4–5).

Are we in the last days? Jesus' words in Matthew 24 give us some clues. Many of the things He talks about in that chapter have not happened yet. But most, if not all, of the conditions that Paul uses to describe the last days in Second Timothy 3 are present-day realities. Like Timothy, we are warned that there will be people who practice forms of Christianity but deny its power. We are told to stay away from such people. Going through the motions of worship without power is draining, depressing, and debilitating. Power is what discriminates between the real and the imposter, the true and the false. Nowhere is the power of God more evident in worship than in the preaching of His word. I am not a seminary professor who teaches homiletics; nor do I desire to look at this subject from that perspective, as valuable and helpful as homiletics can be. But there has never been a time when power in preaching and the corporate gathering of worship have been so desperately needed as the age we are in right now.

POWER THROUGH PREACHING

First, I realize that talking to preachers about preaching can be like a "noisy gong or a clanging cymbal" (1 Cor. 13:1). I have many friends who are US military chaplains who have received an assignment to teach for a year at the Chaplain School at Fort Jackson, South Carolina. The ones who were assigned to teach on the topic of preaching claim it was the worst assignment in their military chaplain careers. Here's why. It's a class that is composed of people who already possess a master of divinity degree, have pastored a church for at least three years, or have extensive experience leading ministry in the mission field. These are the students—attending a mandatory class in a subject they already know, have experience with, and could probably teach better than the teacher can. No wonder it was the worst assignment of their career.

Oblige me now to share some insights from my humble career of being on the platform for four decades, both in the music-leading role as well as in the role of speaking and preaching. And from my ten-year career as a Christian event producer working with some of the top authors and speakers of our time.

POWER IS IN HIS WORDS, NOT OURS

Topical preaching is very popular, and rightly so. Many people want to know the Christian perspective on everything—marriage, family, finances, parenting, how to study the Bible, how to apply biblical principles in business, and on and on. All these subjects are addressed in the Bible through the stories and context of the Bible itself. The power in preaching is not in our words or someone else's words from their latest book on a particular topic. The power in preaching is the Word itself. His Word speaks to every condition of life we face. Except for a few memory verses, people do not know the Bible, its structure, meaning, how and where to get around in it, nor its historical contexts.

Here are two principles for the leader who desires to preach the Word of God with clarity and power. First, recognize that the power is already present within the Word of God.

> For my thoughts are not your thoughts,
>> neither are your ways my ways, declares the LORD.
> For as the heavens are higher than the earth,
>> so are my ways higher than your ways
>> and my thoughts than your thoughts.
> For as the rain and the snow come down from heaven
>> and do not return there but water the earth,
> making it bring forth and sprout,
>> giving seed to the sower and bread to the eater,
> so shall my word be that goes out from my mouth;
>> it shall not return to me empty,
> but it shall accomplish that which I purpose,
>> and shall succeed in the thing for which I sent it.
>
> (Isa. 55:8–11)

We do not need to grunt and groan, hoping something dynamic will happen. The power is already present. The challenges in people's lives today are the same as the forefathers and foremothers of our faith faced. How did they respond? How did they react? What mistakes did they make? How did they handle themselves in righteousness? What happened to their children? How did they deal with sin? Give listeners the power that is already present in the stories, parables, history, and principles found in God's revealed Word.

Second, trust that the Holy Spirit will do the work which He was sent by the Father to do: "These things I have spoken to you while I am still with you. But the Helper, the Holy Spirit, whom the Father will send in my name, he will teach you all things and bring to your remembrance all that I have said to you" (John 14:25–26).

X-MEN AND SUPERWOMEN

The average young churchgoer can tell you the names, actions, failures, and successes of their favorite X-Men and Superwomen from pop culture movies. The characters throughout the Bible need to become the new X-Men and Superwomen talked of throughout the lives of our congregants. The names, actions, failures, and successes of men like Joseph, Nehemiah, Naaman, David, and Onesimus (to name but a random few) possess lessons in topics such as leadership, marriage, employment, finances, and humility. Deborah, Esther, Ruth, Mary, Elizabeth, Priscilla, and Eunice need to become the Superwomen of our young ladies' lives. From this short list, our daughters and wives can learn of faithfulness, boldness, truthfulness, purity, the role of hospitality, the challenges of being the spouse of a clergyman, and being the mother of a young preacher. These are the X-Men and Superwomen we have access to through the Bible. They are the heroes we have the opportunity to lead people to. And because they are the ones included in God's Word, their stories possess the power of Isaiah 55:11 and the assurance of John 14:26.

I encourage youth pastors to do a series on the fathers of the faith, a.k.a. sons and daughters of God's X-Men and Superwomen.

- John and Charles Wesley: Show how they were doing "gospel shows" all over the new colonies, yet had no salvation experience of their own. Talk about hypocrisy. Talk about how God can use us in spite of ourselves. Talk about the power of their ministry after their true conversion. In an age when the zealous of heart are ridiculed, the Wesley story is packed with relevance.
- Augustine of Hippo: Show how this man's thinking and handling of logic became one of the bases for modern ethics and Christian thinking. Look at how that thinking eventually led to Luther.
- Martin Luther: Teach them about the hypocrisy of the church, the corruption of mixing monarchies with religion, why it was important for each man to have and read his own Bible, and how the Reformation changed the church, government, art, and music. Share how worship today is a direct result of Luther's standing solely on the principles of biblical truth. Only after they understand the sixteenth-century Martin Luther does Martin Luther King Jr.'s name bear meaning that is both relevant and risky.

Of course, scriptural exegesis and hero teaching take creativity and preparation. That kind of work takes time. Yet are we not called to do this? Is there power in our preaching? Is there a dryness in our worship? Are we good at using gear, reading the how-to manuals but waffling at the work it takes to dispense truth? The prophet Amos boldly stated what no religious leader in his time wanted to hear: "'Behold, the days are coming,' declares the Lord GOD, / 'when I will send a famine on the land— / not a famine of bread, nor a thirst for water, / but of hearing the words of the LORD'" (Amos 8:11). Do you sense a famine is happening?

You want your congregants asking you: "Where do you get this stuff? It's really good!" This kind of preaching and teaching is what lasts because it is what people remember when they are going through the battles of life. Power in preaching leads to changed hearts. Heart change is the launch pad in people's lives that leads them to worship God in spirit and truth. Not the other way around. Lead them there . . . now.

POWER THROUGH PRAYER

Seventy thousand seats is a lot of seats! It was Friday morning and we were at the Los Angeles Coliseum doing the final sound checks and video tests. Standing on the stage made you feel important, as if you were larger than you really are. The sound cabinets were flown from the steel roofing in a downward spiral that looked like they were ready to blow over the six thousand folding chairs on the field. The screens on both sides of the stage were massive. Yet when you went to the opposite side of the stadium, the stage and all its gear looked very small and insignificant.

As the crews were working to get ready to open the gates, I looked toward the massive span of seats and saw tiny images of people walking through the rows of seventy thousand seats.

"Who are those people out there and what are they doing?" I asked. "That's the prayer team. They touch and pray over every seat before every event," replied one of the volunteers. "All seventy thousand seats?" I asked. "Yup." From its inception, Promise Keepers took its mission seriously. And to their credit, the board of directors and the executive leadership team were convinced that if there was no prayer there was no power.

Do you have a prayer team dedicated to praying over every seat in your place of meeting? Prior to the weekend services? Early on Sunday morning before anyone else arrives? Prayer warriors tend to be soft-spoken people. They don't normally approach a leader to push their prayer agenda. They just pray silently in their closet, and their Father rewards them in silence. Look for those people. Ask others where those people are. The prayer warriors are awaiting their assignments from the leaders. Tap into them and watch God work. What we found and faced in humility was clear: It wasn't our plans that "created moments." It was because of the silent, dedicated, praying warriors who quietly walked each row—touching seventy thousand seats and asking the God of heaven to do His work in the life of whomever would occupy that seat. We were producing a program under their authority. They prayed and God's power was unleashed.

Does your leadership team meet for prayer? Not so much the "pray for my Aunt Tilly in Iowa" prayers—as much as we *do* care about Aunt Tilly! Having been on church staff teams, as well as being a guest for various events, I've seen that prayer can become a quick "nod to God."

In 1996, Promise Keepers hosted the largest gathering of clergy in modern history. The Clergy Conference was a three-day event at the Georgia Dome in Atlanta, GA, which drew over forty thousand clergy from every swath of the Christian faith. The speaker lineup was immense, deep, diverse, and a bit intimidating: Charles Swindoll, Tony Evans, John Maxwell, E.V. Hill, Henry Blackaby, Max Lucado, Jack Hayford, and a myriad of other leaders and authors from all races and denominations. This event was so crucial, controversial, and historic that all of these famous speakers canceled their busy schedules to fly to Colorado for a two-day prayer meeting. If this meeting had not taken place, there would have been no unity of spirit going into this event. The conference would have come off as each speaker arriving, doing their thing, and leaving. The clergy in attendance deserved something more than just another event. They needed and desired God's power—not simply for the conference, but for their ministries, families, and lives.

Okay, so as church worship leaders we aren't planning a gathering of this size—but do we believe the same Jesus is present in power each week when we gather in our local congregations? Do we cancel whatever is on our calendar to gather as a team, simply to humble ourselves, cleanse our hearts and minds, and ask God for His power?

> Again I say to you, if two of you agree on earth about anything they ask, it will be done for them by my Father in heaven. For where two or three are gathered in my name, there am I among them. (Matt. 18:19–20)

> You desire and do not have, so you murder. You covet and cannot obtain, so you fight and quarrel.

> You do not have, because you do not ask. You ask
> and do not receive, because you ask wrongly, to
> spend it on your passions. (James 4:2–3)

Without prayer, all our efforts are equivalent to planning a motivational seminar. We have the gear, the talent, the didactic content, the facility, and the "meat in the seat." The only thing we lack is the presence and power of the One we claim to know and represent. May it never be!

Participation, unpredictability, power. These are the elements that have helped me plan worship that is active, alive, and engaging. Worship that isn't active, alive, and engaging is the equivalent of wallpaper worship. Everyone appreciates it is there, but it is forgotten once they leave the room.

12

THREE ESSENTIALS OF EVALUATION: DECLARE, RESPOND, DEVOTION

Feelings are more dangerous than ideas, because they aren't
susceptible to rational evaluation. They grow quietly, spreading
underground, and erupt suddenly, all over the place.

—Brian Eno

Imagine yourself with your spouse at a romantic dinner in a classy restaurant with soft music, soft lights, white tablecloths, and a candle in the middle of your table for two. The waiter serves your water and wine and gives you the menu for your evening selections. He tells you that he will come back when you are ready to order. You casually look at the menu and chat about the choices. You make your decision and then begin to engage in conversation. The waiter comes back, takes your order, and leaves again. You continue to talk and enjoy one another's company. The waiter returns and interrupts to ask if there is anything he can do for you while you wait for your meal. You say, "No, we're fine, thank you."

He leaves and you resume your conversation. The meal comes and everything is set. You begin to indulge in an expensive but tasty and romantic culinary experience together. As you eat, the waiter continues to interrupt your conversation each time he returns to pour water. He even joins by asking you questions and lingering at your table. Annoying, right? Would he not serve his customers better by simply leaving them to their romantic conversation?

This is what happens when a worship leader effectively leads the congregation into a place of worship intimacy, but for some reason feels he or she is supposed to keep going. Lead where? We are here! Once led to a place of intimacy, congregants may want to be left alone there for a moment. Any further leading is as annoying as a waiter interrupting during a romantic dinner.

These kinds of insights on "how we are doing what we are doing" can only come from outside evaluation. I don't know about you, but I hate seeing myself on video. It reveals everything I'm doing wrong. The worst part is, I didn't know I was doing "that thing." It could be anything from scratching my face to contorting my mouth in an annoying way. Or, even worse, when evaluating my speaking, that I repeated what I just said and then repeated it again. Everyone sees it. I don't. That's true in life too. Video is a way to see ourselves truthfully, as others see us. The stark reality is that we may be acting just like an annoying waiter and not even know it. Whether we are musicians, speakers, preachers, or liturgists assisting on the platform, evaluating what we do is crucial to becoming better at what we do.

This is also true of worship services themselves. A truthful way to know what actually happened and how it came off is to watch a video of the service. The problem with that is it takes time during the following week, time that we would rather spend planning and preparing for the next event.

I use a three-pronged approach to evaluate any program I am planning—*before* it is executed and while it is still on paper. I learned these three essentials from Buddy Owens, who was the Maranatha! Music head producer for the Promise Keepers events. I heard Buddy share these elements of evaluation during one of Maranatha! Music's workshops, and I have found them helpful ever since. These "Essential Elements of Evaluation" will not only help you in your overall program evaluation, but will also help you with the following challenges, which face any leader of worship—musical or otherwise:

- Choosing songs
- Choosing program elements
- Making elements flow together in a logical manner

You can design any service or program, look at it on paper, and use the three essential elements of evaluation to get a feel for:

- What's happening
- Why it's happening
- Why you put it where you put it in the flow
- How it serves the overall purpose
- How it interacts with the other elements for the good of the whole program
- Why it may need to be moved to a different place in the flow or even be deleted

The three elements of evaluation are declare, respond, and devotion.

Each element in your service will fall under one of these three categories. Each song, each reading, each moment in the service accomplishes something unique. It either *declares* something, or it is a *response* to something that was declared. *Devotion* is the moment we all want to see happen. It is that point in the service when we allow congregants to have a moment of spiritual intimacy, which may result in a commitment or a changed heart.

Now before we go any further, let me reiterate something I said in the previous chapter. This is not about creating a powerful moment. Without prayer, there is no power. Without submission to God's authority, His word, and His spirit, we are planning and pulling off the equivalent of a motivational seminar or pep rally. That said, there is great value in evaluating the whys, the whats, and the whats behind the whys. Let's march forward together in humility.

Break all three of these elements of evaluation down and see how much of what you are doing in your services declares, facilitates, and becomes that moment of devotion. The idea is to look at the last service you led, consider every element of the service, and make a note beside each element (song choice, reading, liturgy, video, announcements, sacraments). Did it *declare* God's character, His glory, His works? Or was the element a *response*: our praise for His character, our joy of His salvation, our wonder at the work of His hands? Then find the moment(s) of *devotion*—those intimate, personal experiences that are allowed to take place. You may realize it didn't happen, or that you are not allowing space for a moment of devotion to happen. These three categories of evaluation will help you see what you are doing and why you are doing it. They will help you recognize the natural flow of your service and reveal if your planning is producing the results that you and your team desire. They may show you why your service seems disjointed and, based on that discovery, may lead you to make changes that are needed.

DECLARE

The first priority in a worship service is to *declare*. We choose elements to open the service that will publically and corporately declare one or more of the following:

- Who we are worshipping
- Who God is and what He has done
- What He is like: His attributes, His character, His power, His greatness, etc.

This can be done using any number of tools in your toolbox:

- Scripture reading
- Call to worship
- Video
- Song or set of songs

To be specific, here are some examples of Scriptures that declare:

- "The heavens are telling of the glory of God; / And their expanse is declaring the work of His hands" (Ps. 19:1, NASB).
- "The LORD is gracious and merciful; / Slow to anger and great in lovingkindness. / The LORD is good to all, / And His mercies are over all His works" (145:8–9, NASB).

There are hundreds of verses that declare the glory and greatness of God. It is fun and fulfilling to dig in and find them, and then use them to craft the portions of your service that will declare His character and His works.

In comparison, here are some Scriptures that are great for other purposes but do not declare:

- "Create in me a clean heart, O God, / And renew a steadfast spirit within me" (51:10, NASB). This is a famous and great passage, but it falls closer to the category of devotion. The emphasis of this passage is on an individual's sin and the need to become clean. There will be a place in the service for that, but the opening portion is not that place.
- "Blessed is the man / who walks not in the counsel of the wicked, . . . / but his delight is in the law of the LORD" (Ps. 1:1–2). I absolutely love this psalm. But it doesn't work to declare because the subject is man.

Hopefully you get the idea.

Here are some song ideas that declare:

- "A Mighty Fortress Is Our God"
- "All Hail the Power of Jesus' Name"
- "Holy, Holy, Holy, Lord God Almighty"

As I side note, I am choosing hymns simply because they are generally more well-known and universally used, even in contemporary settings. There are many contemporary songs that fit each of our three categories, but the problem is they will be dated and unused in a few years. So, for the sake of our examples, let's stay with songs that have stood the test of time and denominational usage.

The songs above are examples that contain lyrics that declare the power, majesty, and works of the Lord, with little or no reference to human experience, opinion, or feeling.

Here are a few songs that are great, but again, they don't fall into the category of declaring:

- "Amazing Grace"
- "Be Thou My Vision"

When we examine the lyrical content of "Amazing Grace," we find it to be more responsive than declarative: "Amazing grace! How sweet the sound, that saved a wretch like me / I once was lost but now I'm found / T'was blind but now I see." In this first verse alone, the person singing the song ("I" or "me") is referred to four times, and a fifth time indirectly ("T'was blind" infers "I was blind, but now I see.") The same is true in "Be Thou My Vision": "Be Thou my vision / O Lord of my heart / Naught be all else to me save that Thou art / Thou my best thought by day or by night / Waking or sleeping Thy treasure, my light." Count how many references to self are present in the lyrics, and it will give you a pretty good clue that the song is not necessarily one that declares the works of God. These are great examples of responsive or even devotional tools (more on those categories ahead).

Whether it is a song selection or a Scripture reading or a piece of liturgy, the idea is that the tool you use is for the purpose of declaring the works of God, period—*His* works, *His* greatness, *His* creation, *His* salvation.

RESPONSE

After we have declared the greatness of God and established fully that He is the reason we have gathered and He is the object of our worship, we can then *respond* to what we have declared. This is praise at its essence. Praising God for who He is and what He has done is our response.

Psalm 8:3-9 contains a passage that *declares*, followed by a passage that *responds*. The declaration is in verses 3–8.

When I look at your heavens, the work of your fingers,
    the moon and the stars, which you have set in place,
what is man that you are mindful of him,
    and the son of man that you care for him?
Yet you have made him a little lower than the heavenly beings
    and crowned him with glory and honor.
You have given him dominion over the works of your hands;
    you have put all things under his feet,
all sheep and oxen,
    and also the beasts of the field,
the birds of the heavens, and the fish of the sea,
    whatever passes along the paths of the seas.

The response is in verse 9.

O Lord, our Lord,
    how majestic is your name in all the earth!

Psalm 9:1-2 continues the response.

> I will give thanks to the LORD with my whole heart;
>> I will recount all of your wonderful deeds.
> I will be glad and exult in you;
>> I will sing praise to your name, O Most High.

So the idea is that to declare gives us something to which we respond. A great worship experience follows this pattern: declare – respond – declare – respond – declare – respond. And this pattern can go on as long as you want in your service.

Songs that are repsonsive are plentiful and actually easier to find than those that declare. The Wesleyan hymn "And Can It Be, That I Should Gain?" actually does both. The verses declare and the refrain responds.

Verse 2:
He left His Father's throne above,
So free, so infinite His grace;
Emptied Himself of all but love,
And bled for Adam's helpless race;
'Tis mercy all, immense and free;
For, O my God, it found out me.

Refrain:
Amazing love! How can it be
That Thou, my God, should die for me!

Verse 4:
No condemnation now I dread;
Jesus, and all in Him is mine!

Alive in Him, my living Head,
And clothed in righteousness divine,
Bold I approach the eternal throne,
And claim the crown, through Christ my own.

Refrain:
Amazing love! How can it be
That Thou, my God, should die for me![1]

Even though there are references to *I* or *mine*, the thrust of the lyrics leans on the immenseness of what God has done for the individual. The verses are *His* story, which has become *mine*. The refrain is sheer response to what we have declared in the verses.

Learn to choose program elements that respond to what has been declared. To start with a response assumes that everyone in the congregation has already had an experience with God for which they are grateful. This is a huge assumption and risks losing an opportunity to declare something about God in the presence of people who may never have given any thought to the great works of this God they are worshipping. *After* we have declared, our response makes sense.

DEVOTION

Devotion is that intimate moment which the overattentive waiter destroyed in the restaurant! (See also Appendix E: "The Larry Norman Story.") The moment of devotion is the moment that transcends all others. It is the point in the service everything else has led to. It can be quiet, but it doesn't have to be quiet. It can appear once, or in a variety of places within the service. For the sake of evaluation and planning, let's say for the average worship service (lasting sixty to ninety minutes), there can be one to three moments of devotion. Here's where to look for that moment in your service:

- After a sermon
- During or after Communion
- In a time of prayer or reflection

The moment of devotion is one that has to be allowed to happen, not forced or manipulated to happen. It can be ambiguous and unpredictable. It is a holy moment when hearts are knit with the Spirit of God. A tear falls. A memory is healed. Forgiveness flows. A truth hits home. A commitment is whispered. A stake is driven into the ground.

The key is to not quench the moment of devotion. If it happens, it has a life of its own. It may not take long, but it can feel like an eternity. Giving devotion its place in worship is paramount. If congregants understand where they've been led, and are allowed to enjoy its reality, they will become faithful and dedicated worshippers. This is the authenticity they are looking for. This is the reason they come back. This is why they will be motivated to bring family members or friends.

We must recognize the importance of devotion and give it its place within the worship context.

Following are some examples of Scripture that can serve the purpose of devotion. These passages reflect the human condition and its desperate need for God:

- "Create in me a clean heart, O God, / and renew a right spirit within me" (Ps. 51:10).
- "For I am already being poured out as a drink offering, and the time of my departure has come. I have fought the good fight, I have finished the race, I have kept the faith" (2 Tim. 4:6–7).
- "Come to me, all who labor and are heavy laden, and I will give you rest" (Matt. 11:28).
- "As a deer pants for flowing streams, / so pants my soul for you, O God. / My soul thirsts for God, / for the living God. / When shall I come and appear before God?" (Ps. 42:1–2).

The history of song in worship reveals that times of political and religious struggle produce more subjectivity and personal devotion in song lyrics. Following the Thirty Years War of Europe (1618-1648) "reliance on an omnipotent God for comfort and consolation was written into the hymns of this period, producing expressions of Christian devotion and individual self-consciousness."[2] There are so many songs today that reflect personal DEVOTION there is not room to list them.

Here are a few hymns. Make sure you take time to look at the lyrical content of these hymns (found in Appendix F) so you understand why they are devotional:

- "Be Thou My Vision"
- "It Is Well with My Soul"
- "Take My Life and Let It Be"
- "Amazing Grace"

Let me point out that devotion is not simply about using slower tempo songs. For instance "Revelation Song" (Jennie Lee Riddle,

Gateway Create Publishing) is a slow tempo, reflective song. But its lyrics are not devotional. They are responsive. "In Christ Alone" (Keith Getty and Stuart Townend, Thankyou Music) is a slow tempo song, but it is declarative. Conversely, "Amazing Grace" has been contemporized in the version known as "Grace Like Rain" and can really rock, but it is still effective as a repsonse or devotion tool. Proper use of the tools will build the house accurately.

PLACEMENT IS EVERYTHING

You may find, after this evaluation, that some of your elements are misplaced. It's okay to change where they appear in the flow of your service. In fact, if you change them according to these three essential elements, you will find your service flows better. Your people will notice the changes. Sure, some will just notice that there have been a few things switched around. Others will notice when the depth of their worship experience expands because of the changes. Listen to those people.

PLACEMENT GONE WILD

Where the elements of a worship service are placed is absolutely paramount. Placement can make or break a service. Here are some examples of misplaced elements. Unfortunately, they are commonplace:

- A meaningful moment followed by announcements
- Communion rushed to save time
- Sermons unprepared, un-prayed over, uninspiring, or too complex (or all of the above)

- Music that is all new and thus all unfamiliar
- The worship (music) leader leading the band but leaving congregants behind
- A service style so flippant or casual it can no longer be called worship
- Relying on the music (its style, tempo, key, or performance) to "create" worship (review chapter 8)

Here are some additional points of evaluation for your planning. Some of these I have already mentioned:

- Be aware of what comes *before* and what comes *after* each element of your service.
- Examine your service structure. Use DRD evaluation to make it flow intelligently.
- Consider the context of the service. What kind of service is it?
  - o   Weekly service based on sermon series or calendar
  - o   Lent or Advent, Easter or Christmas
  - o   Special – funeral/celebration/wedding
- Choose songs that are appropriate.
  - o   Content (What is the song saying?)
  - o   Context (Does it fit here? Use DRD.)

PITCH PLACEMENT
(FOR MUSICAL WORSHIP LEADERS)

In the spirit of making singing accessible to everyone, I encourage lead singers to try to pitch the songs they lead in a key that makes singing easy for most people. For instance, just last Sunday morning the man leading the singing was straining to reach the notes in the melody that were out of his range. Well, I too was reaching, trying to sing along from the congregation. I wondered why they didn't try a different key for the song, especially as I spotted the guitar player playing with a capo on the neck of the guitar—a sure sign that the song could've been played with the same chords in a much lower key that would've been more singable. (Don't worry if that didn't make sense to you, if you're not a musician.) The point is: If the song is making the leaders strain to reach the notes, it is likely making the congregation strain to reach them too. This is why it is crucial to know your musical craft. Being able to play in a number of keys is crucial to putting the songs in a singing range that is accessible to those who are being led. Simply because a musical source like YouTube or a compact disc recording has a song in one key, does not mean musicians cannot transpose it to a different key. Volunteer musicians may be limited in their ability to do this, but it is a crucial skill to learn.

I encourage leaders to key songs in keys men can sing. The reason for this is because women traditionally love to sing and will sing anyway. They just will! If men find the song(s) unsingable for their voice, they will not participate. If the men participate, the women will too. They already are. Try to use keys which altos or baritones can sing in.

WHAT DO WE DO WITH THOSE DOGGONE HYMNS?

I am asked this question in almost every worship workshop I lead. Let me address this briefly on a couple of levels.

Most of the musicians who attend my worship workshops are from contemporary congregations, many of whom are self-taught. It is important to understand that the hymns, as they have appeared in hymnbooks for hundreds of years, were written in four-part choral style known as SATB (soprano, alto, tenor, bass). That style works for a cappella singing in parts, by singers who actually read music, and for piano or organ accompaniment. Every church from the late middle ages until the late 1960s sang the hymns in SATB style. Obviously, the hymn-writers and subsequent church music publishers were unaware that by the late twentieth century local church musicians would be, for the most part, self-taught rock and roll guitarists and keyboardists. This repertoire of hymns simply doesn't work with our contemporary rhythm sections, unless some serious musical surgery is performed to make them work. Most band musicians would rather not bother, and I get that. But in my experience it doesn't have to be all or nothing—or either/or. Many of these hymns can work with a rhythm section. Notice I said *many*, not *all*. The key is to know how to choose the ones that can work. When a hymn comes together with our modern way of producing music, the results can create a powerful experience. Plus, since worship is our heritage, we want to introduce that heritage to new believers and upcoming generations by making sure we are passing on the inheritance.

Here's how:

1. Learn the melody.

Don't worry about the harmonies in the SATB arrangement in a hymnbook. Just concentrate on learning the melody alone. Today, songwriters usually write their lyrics and the melodies at the same time. The truth is that the melodies of many of the hymns were matched to the lyrics later by a composer who was unknown to the hymnwriter. (Saint Francis of Assisi's poem "All Creatures of Our God and King" was set to its current melody four hundred years after Saint Francis wrote it.)

2. Find a chord pattern that matches what you are singing.

Use a guitar or a piano to do this. After you have found something you think works, play (or have someone else play) the original SATB style. This will help you identify where you should change your new chords to better match the original musical idea behind the hymn. Why is this important? For the same reason that when musicians "cover" a song, they try to do it as close to the original as possible so as to not throw the listener off—or even tick the listener off! Again, it's about inviting the congregants into something familiar, even if it is a fresh version of something very ancient.

3. If there are more than four verses, edit it down to two or three.

Be careful with this process because you're messing with someone else's lyrics, ideas, and creativity. But also know that some verses in older hymns were added by tradition, long after the hymnwriter was gone. If eliminating a verse or two does not change the overall message of the song, you're fine. Beware of "A Mighty Fortress Is Our God." The third verse ends where the fourth verse begins. So to skip the third verse makes the fourth verse sound ridiculous:

> Verse 3:
> And though this world, with devils filled,
> Should threaten to undo us,
> We will not fear, for God has willed
> His truth to triumph through us.
> The prince of darkness grim,
> We tremble not for him,
> His rage we can endure,
> For lo, his doom is sure,
> One little word shall fell him.
>
> Verse 4:
> That word above all earthly powers ...[3]

See what I mean? If you skipped verse three and went straight to verse four, you just led your congregants into a moment of ambiguous ignorance. Just do your research.

4. Some hymns can rock, some cannot.

Beware of hymns that change chords with every word. Most of the culprits I've found are from the English hymnody tradition: Wesley hymns which include some Christmas carols—for example, "O Come All Ye Faithful," "God Rest Ye Merry Gentlemen," and many others. The trick is to find the ones that match your DRD (declare, respond, devotion) first. Then, as you work with each hymn, you'll realize if they work musically or not. One trick may be to not use the whole band but only a guitar, keys, and a special instrument (flute or violin). Then *season* it with percussion instead of using a full drum kit.

5. Some hymns need to be left alone. Some need to be left out.

There are many great devotion-oriented hymns that work well in their slow tempo ballad forms. For instance, when I hear "Be Thou My Vision" played in the traditional setting, it is clunky and uninteresting. But when the same hymn is done with a small rhythm section, it is charming, meaningful, and (I believe) closer to what the composer intended. This is true because the melody is actually an Irish folk melody, so it works well with folkie instruments. It was never meant to be played by a pipe organ and sung in SATB choral style. But there are many hymns that simply don't need to be messed with or rocked out. They just need to be sung. "Take My Life and Let It Be," "It Is Well with My Soul," and "Amazing Grace" are a few examples. There are many, many other great ones. (Refer to appendixes A and B.)

There are also some that need to be left out completely. I have run across some hymns sung by my parent's generation that I disagree with theologically. Again, DRD is a great tool for vetting, not only hymns but also contemporary songs. Not everything that is being thrown into the market works well for congregational use. Nor is everything being published necessarily accurate theologically.

FOR SPEAKERS AND MUSICIANS: LET YOURSELF GROW IN YOUR CRAFT

It is imperative that church musicians grow musically. It is simply too limiting to have been exposed to only one style of music—contemporary Christian or modern worship. I am constantly encouraging young musicians to go to a college they can afford and study music legitimately. The years invested there will pay huge dividends later. I have run into too many church music people who can rock well, know gear, and can put together chord charts for a band. But they have no idea how to hear whether a flute or a cello would work better in a song, much less how to write a part for another instrument. I have run into many who have had no exposure to mainstream pop or rock music or jazz because they were raised on the premise that anything outside the church was considered secular or evil. I understand the motive to keep oneself unstained from the world. But keeping oneself unstained is different from keeping oneself uneducated.

Many large churches are tired of music people who are "one trick ponies," who know only one style of music. Some are laying off their band performers and trading them in for trained musicians who not only know how to lead a band, but also have the musical background to oversee musical theater, an orchestra, a choral program—or at least know where to hire those who can, and know enough to vet those who apply for the jobs. The times may be a-changin' again. Just as pastors and corporate leaders have to do ongoing education, musicians need to choose to grow musically.

Likewise, pastors and leaders who are called upon to speak publically also need to be willing to grow in their craft. Many of the skills needed in speaking are taught in seminary and honed with experience. Having worked with some of the most popular speakers in the nation, I was impressed by how many were still students of their craft—desiring to improve, self-critique, and become better at communicating to their audiences. Here are a few tips I picked up from the pros:

1. Speak from a position of weakness, not strength. Audiences resent being talked down to, as if the speaker is one who has flawlessly put every principle he/she is espousing into action. Share stories of personal failure, instead of pointing the finger at others' failures. Vulnerability is believable.

2. Read your audience and be ready to adjust as they respond to you. This is the essence of "using your binoculars."

3. Keep it simple. I remember my mentor, Tom Hemingway, who had a bazillion war stories. Yet his talking points were simple, clear, and few. His stories were used only to make a point and then move on. The late great Dr. Howard Hendricks taught, "If it's a mist in the pulpit, it's a fog in the congregation!" Keep it simple and clear.

4. Evaluate yourself and ask others for their input. I worked with one pastor who had great content but his delivery was peppered throughout with "and by the way . . ." He was constantly going off on rabbit trails. The reason he kept doing this is simple: He never allowed anyone to speak into his craft, nor would he ever watch himself on video. Vince Lombardi said, "The difference between a successful person and others is not a lack of strength, not a lack of knowledge, but rather a lack of will." Your audience deserves the best you have and you haven't discovered the best you have yet. Get over it and go for it!

A FINAL WORD ON EVALUATION

After you have written the headings beside each piece you have used in the past few services, ask yourself: "How does it flow? Does it make sense? Why are we doing that at this point in the service?" Did you identify *where* you are leading your people? Do you know where the goal line is? Are you leading them to a moment of devotion? Is the Holy Spirit meeting you, your leadership team, and your people at that moment? Or is what you are doing feeling stiff or contrived? If it is, go back and read chapters 9 and 10. Find the essence of what you feel you are missing. Ask God to lead *you*, the leader. Go through this evaluation process with your ministry team. Observe their responses. Listen to what they *are* saying as well as what they *are not* saying.

Always remember, the last thing you want is for your congregants to sit there or stand there, doing nothing but listening to you. You want them to be present in the moment. You want them *with* you. The more they participate with you, the more they can trust you to take them someplace intimate with the Lord. If you don't care whether or not they are with you, but simply want to pull off a great performance, you probably should be playing in a nightclub. But if you are a leader of worship—whether musical or otherwise—engage your followers with integrity and purpose.

13

OUR LEGACY OF WORSHIP: WHAT WILL WE PASS ON?

When you have eaten and are satisfied and have built good hous-
es and lived in them, your silver and gold multiply and all you
have multiplies, then your heart will become proud and you will
forget the Lord your God.

Deuteronomy 8:12–14, NASB

Television sitcoms are often filmed without a live audience, which is why directors use prerecorded laugh tracks to give the viewer guidance on when and how to react. It creates a false feeling of community to laugh along with an anonymous and even nonexistent audience. Wallpaper worship produces a similar isolated experience. It is the result of a gap between the platform and the people. When congregants do not participate, whoever is on the stage is observed as if they are the television studio talent acting for an audience they cannot see. What should be an uplifting experience becomes a voyeuristic and disconnected nonexperience. It's odd to call something like that "worship."

I have attended church worship seminars led by guest speakers and authors who taught musicians and church leaders that they need to align themselves with the latest technology and cultural trends to keep their congregations in step with the most recent advances in worship arts and sciences. The fundamental assumption of those seminars is that people cannot worship unless they are taught how. I disagree.

Worship is organic. It is as natural as breathing. When a baby is born, it begins taking in air instead of amniotic fluid. They do it without instruction, direction, or example. They don't have to attend a class to be taught how to breathe. Worship is like that. It is not something we learn; it is something we do naturally. One does not have to look far to see people worshipping their favorite athletic team, popular musician, Hollywood stars, or even comfort food. We are made to worship and the fact that humans worship something, anything, makes the point. Do people go to seminars to be trained on how to adore their favorite actor or to learn the latest techniques of "fangirling?"

The logical next question to ask then is "What or whom do you worship?" Blogs and church platforms are rife with well-intentioned writers and preachers who repeat the mantra, "Where you spend your time or money indicates who or what you are worshipping." I understand the intent behind that thought, but it usually ends up only shaming the hearer. Instead of asking, "Are we worshipping?" perhaps a more relevant question is "Why are we worshipping what we are worshipping?"

Just as we are created by God to organically worship, we are endowed with an innate desire to worship together. We want to be a part of something larger than ourselves. We want to belong.

"Let us consider how to stimulate one another to love and good deeds, not forsaking our own assembling together, as is the habit of some, but encouraging one another; and all the more as you see the day drawing near" (Heb. 10: 24–25, NASB).

Love and good deeds are not things we express to ourselves, but to others. They do not find their expression from an individual experience that is isolated or passively observed. They are the fruit of truly corporate and participatory worship that points us outward.

OUR LEGACY OF WORSHIP

As societies and cultures change, so do the styles through which those cultures express themselves. That which was once considered new and fresh eventually becomes old and traditional. Unless we can draw back and see ourselves in historical context, we can get caught up in doing it the same way it was always done. When it came to the music portion of the Protestant worship experience, my parent's generation looked like an organ on one side, a piano on the other, and a choir in the middle. My generation looked like a few guitars that were snuck onto the platform. This generation looks like a full rock rhythm section with a couple of singers holding microphones with in-ear monitors—surrounded by moving lights, colored fog, and massive screens, with shoulder camera operators moving in and out of the people on the platform. All generations eventually say the same thing: "We've always done it like this." When the form of expression eclipses what is attempting to be expressed, the questions start flying. When the hows of worship become more important than the whys of worship, we have missed the point of worship itself. I personally do not think this is what anyone in the body of Christ wants. But history proves it is a common trap that causes each generation in the church to stumble.

WHAT WILL WE PASS ON?

Are our children experiencing us experiencing God? Are they witnessing their parents participating in worship? Or are they watching us watch others? I have witnessed children using smartphones and tablets, while their parents stand and passively observe musicians on the platform or on large video screens. We have friends who attend three different congregations: one for the youth/children's program, one for preaching, and one for the entertainment quotient. We know many committed believers who have given up going to church altogether and have chosen to gather in a small home group. A close friend of mine, a longtime Christian, recently said, "Going to church for me is like buying cotton candy at the ballgame: It looks great; but when you bite into it, you bite your own lip because there is actually more air than substance." Ouch!

As Christians, our excellence is not in our abilities as musicians, orators, authors, or production managers. Our excellence is what the Scriptures refer to as "the hidden person of the heart" (1 Pet. 3:4; see also 1 Sam. 16:7). Without a love for God and His people, which transforms how we lead from the platform, the Scriptures remind us that we are as a "noisy gong or a clanging cymbal" (1 Cor. 13:1). In other words, we may look good, sound good, and even fill the parking lot. But if those are the criteria we use to judge what we are doing, we may have our excellence-emphasis in the wrong place.

When I lived in Nashville, I had the opportunity to interact personally with one of the most successful record producers in history. He and his wife had temporarily moved into the rental house across the street from us in Franklin, Tennessee, while waiting for their custom home to be built. It gave us the opportunity to get to know them, to "ooh and aah" over the names of some of the famous musicians this man had produced. The walls of his house were lined with platinum and gold record awards. He had also won Dove awards (the Christian music version of a Grammy award) for producing some very popular Christian recordings. Oddly, he was an avowed non-Christian. He was well-read, intelligent, and treated us with dignity and respect, offering production advice and even free time at his downtown Nashville studio. But he had no desire to explore Christianity, even after he had been awarded as a top Christian record producer. I asked him why he wasn't a Christian. His answer was, "You people are simply wanting the same thing everyone else in the music industry wants."

When people attend worship services we have planned and executed, are they leaving thinking, "You people are simply wanting what everyone else wants?" Do they see our efforts in production, lighting, sound, public speaking, music, performance, organization, church-growth goal setting, ushering, traffic control, parking, building projects, marketing, and barista techniques as rungs on the same success ladder they are climbing?

Does a full church parking lot indicate that what is going on inside is something different than any other event in an arena, auditorium, or beach band shell? When the church parking lot is full but the mouths of those inside are empty, it's time we ask: What's wrong with this picture?

A LEGACY OF HUMILITY

I recently heard a two-star naval rear admiral, who happened to be a committed Christian, describe how his week is filled with meetings, protocol, and nonstop activity. He is constantly surrounded by people who need his input, desire his approval, and await his every decision. He is contacted by Congress, called into conversations with full four-star admirals, and privy to highly classified information. He began to describe how his weekend starts. He is driven to his residence by his driver, while his aide briefs him in the back seat, giving him his weekend assignments to complete at home. The car pulls up to his residence and the driver walks around to open the back door of the admiral's car. The aide gets out first, checking the street to make sure it is safe for the admiral to leave the car. The admiral then climbs out of the back seat. He returns the salutes of his aide and driver and walks up to the front door of his residence. The driver and aide wait for the admiral to enter his house and close the door. The driver and aide then get back into the vehicle and drive away. As the admiral removes his uniform hat, his wife approaches with a kitchen trash bag in hand. "This needs to go outside. And after you get out of your uniform the kitty litter needs to be changed."

Humility is a hallmark of a godly person. No matter what rank we have achieved, our lives are still about living life, day in and day out. The Scriptures are very clear on how God views pride and arrogance.

> God opposes the proud but gives grace to the humble. (James 4:6)

> He regards the lowly,
>> but the haughty he knows from afar.
>>> (Ps. 138:6)

> Behold, I am against you, O proud one
>> declares the Lord God of hosts,
> for your day has come.
>>> (Jer. 50:31)

If we lack humility, we have set ourselves in opposition to God. We may think we are doing His work. But if our work and our lives are laced with arrogance, God is actually in opposition to our lives and our work.

Moses learned this the hard way. He was so frustrated with God and the stubborn people he was leading, that when God commanded him to *speak* to the rock in order for it to pour forth water, Moses *struck* the rock with his staff instead, in arrogant disobedience. By hauling off and hitting the rock, against God's will, Moses set himself in opposition to God. The penalty for his behavior came later, when Moses was not allowed to enter into the Promised Land with the people he had led (see Num. 20:2–13). Recently, I was working backstage at one of the largest churches in Denver, tuning their piano (piano tuning is

one of my "tentmaking" income streams) to get them ready
for Easter services. While I was working, a meeting of the
creative production team was being held in a room off to
the side. I heard one of the lead pastors yelling at his team,
"People, wake up! Easter is only two weeks away!" I wondered how those team members felt hearing their leader
coming unglued. I wondered about the effectiveness of this
kind of intimidation in a setting that was supposed to be
wrought with humility and kindness. I wondered if the
pastor had set himself in opposition to God. I wondered
if God's Spirit showed up there on Easter Sunday. I wondered how many other church leaders were yelling at their
staff members prior to the biggest production event of their
year. I wondered how many churches would be pulling off
massive Easter services in opposition to the God they were
representing. I also remembered the times I have violated
the same principles I am espousing here.

I was booked four years in a row to lead the worship
team for the Hawaiian Island Ministries annual conference
in Honolulu. Prior to inviting me, there had never been a
worship leader asked back that many times in a row. I was
so proud of myself. But it all came crashing down during
the fourth year, when my product merchandise tables were
not in a prominent place in the lobby of the conference center. I came unglued and complained to the workers. I got
so bent out of shape, my anger came out on the platform.
I made some snide remarks in between worship songs that
killed any hope of my being asked back. Humility. "God is
not mocked, for whatever one sows, that will he also reap"
(Gal. 6:7).

A LEGACY OF INTEGRITY

My mentor, Marine Lt. Colonel Tom Hemingway, once told me, "Honesty is not integrity. Honesty is a *result* of integrity." (The US Marine Corps slogan is "Semper Fidelis": Always Faithful.) We get the word *integrity* from the root word *integrate*, meaning wholeness or completeness. Integration yields honesty. Living in an integrated way means living one life, not living a double life.

In chapter 6, I talked about how worship is not casual. Leading a congregation of people into the worship experience—through music, preaching, liturgy, or any other tool—is not something we do in a drunken state of mind or a compromised state of heart. The passage about sowing and reaping (Gal. 6:7–8) is simply a reflection of a natural law God set in motion in Genesis 8:22, following the flood: "While the earth remains, seedtime and harvest, cold and heat, summer and winter, day and night, shall not cease." In other words, the consequences of sin are automatic and unavoidable. Believe me, I know. Will we leave a legacy of integrity?

It's time to evaluate where we are and how we got here. If we don't stop what we are doing and start asking probing questions, we may miss being a part of a transformation of the church into an active, participating, responsive group of believers, who start looking more like Mary than Martha (see Luke 10:38–42).

MY HOUSE

When I reflect on wallpaper worship, where during a worship service (a) 80 percent of the congregants passively provide an audience for performers on the platform, or (b) one third of the congregants head to the lobby for coffee, or (c) meaningful ancient rituals cause people to fall into a deep slumber, I find myself thinking, *What would Jesus do if He were here physically?* One of the most chilling moments in Jesus' journey is when He enters the temple in Jerusalem and sees the state of affairs.

> And he entered the temple and began to drive out those who sold and those who bought in the temple, and he overturned the tables of the money-changers and the seats of those who sold pigeons. And he would not allow anyone to carry anything through the temple. And he was teaching them and saying to them, "Is it not written, 'My house shall be called a house of prayer for all the nations'? But you have made it a den of robbers." (Mark 11:15–17)

In verse 17, Jesus is quoting from the prophets Isaiah and Jeremiah in the same sentence.

> These [people] I will bring to my holy mountain,
>   and make them joyful in my house of prayer;
> their burnt offerings and their sacrifices
>   will be accepted on my altar;
> for my house shall be called a house of prayer
>   for all peoples.
>   (Isa. 56:7)

> Has this house, which is called by my name, be-
> come a den of robbers in your eyes? Behold, I my-
> self have seen it, declares the LORD. (Jer. 7:11)

Matthew, Mark, and Luke's telling of this scene in the Temple, which is traditionally referred to as "Jesus' Cleansing of The Temple," consistently report Jesus' quotes in a somewhat benign fashion: "He was teaching them and saying to them" (Mark 11:17) or simply: "He said to them" (Matt. 21:13). Some recent movies that portray this scene have the character of Jesus screaming these Isaiah/Jeremiah quotes in anger, as He is simultaneously overturning tables and opening dove cages. They show the doves flying out, goats and sheep running loose around the Temple, coins of merchants flying everywhere, people running to take cover—you get the picture. I wonder what Jesus would say if he were to walk into one of our twenty-first-century church facilities and experience wallpaper worship?

We looked earlier at Nehemiah and his priest Ezra, and their calling together of the nation of Israel to dedicate themselves, following their return from Babylonian exile. Nehemiah's vision was to return to Jerusalem to rebuild the city wall after it had been torn down and the city pillaged for seventy years. The worship service which Nehemiah called for and Ezra led—reading of the law, confession of sin, and rejoicing over God's faithfulness—was their dedication worship service of the wall of Jerusalem. The next job was to rebuild the Temple. The Temple was where God's manifest presence would dwell among them. It was to be a place of beauty and holiness, meticulously rebuilt to God's specs, and also dedicated as "a house of prayer for all peoples." This period, following Nehemiah, was a time of blessing, prosperity, and a renewed identity for Israel in their old home of Jerusalem. They were no longer slaves in Babylon, but a people who were free to worship their God in a temple they were to rebuild. But the people got distracted from temple rebuilding and instead built beautiful, comfortable homes for themselves. It is during this time that the prophet Haggai shows up to give a word to the leaders of Israel.

> Is it a time for you yourselves to dwell in your paneled houses, while this house lies in ruins? Now, therefore, thus says the LORD of hosts: Consider your ways. You have sown much, and harvested little. You eat, but you never have enough; you drink, but you never have your fill. You clothe yourselves, but no one is warm. And he who earns wages does so to put them into a bag with holes. (Hag. 1:4–6)

Haggai continues:

> Thus says the LORD of hosts: Consider your ways. Go up to the hills and bring wood and build the house, that I may take pleasure in it and that I may be glorified, says the LORD. You looked for much, and behold, it came to little. And when you brought it home, I blew it away. Why? declares the LORD of hosts. Because of my house that lies in ruins, while each of you busies himself with his own house. (1:7–9)

Though these stories of the Temple (Jesus in Jerusalem and Haggai's prophecies) are about events that happened a very long time ago, it is crucial for you and me to see the correlation between God's desire for His house and our role in fulfilling His desire for His house. Does God view His house today as being in ruins while we busy ourselves with wallpaper worship?

I relate to the setting of Haggai's message. It is in times of prosperity and when things seem to be going well that I let down my guard and get distracted from the important work to which God has called me. The disciplines that keep me on track—prayer, personal reflection, listening instead of speaking, giving of time and resources—can become routine and mundane when compared to the flashy and more attractive things I find myself wanting to do. My sense of self-importance rises, while my daily walk with Christ wanes. Then I pray for humility or renewed spirituality. Instead of receiving those characteristics in a nicely wrapped package conveniently placed at my doorstep, I get events and situations that confront my arrogance and prove me lacking. Maybe that is what it means to "walk in the light, as he is in the light" (1 John 1:7). I begin to see things as they really are in the light, and it is not always pleasant.

As painful as it can be, it seems we learn our deepest and most valuable lessons of being Christlike through seasons of hardship or suffering. I don't like that. Christian friends of mine would agree; they don't like it either. But it seems to be a consistent way through which we learn to become true worshippers of God, rather than lip-service worshippers (see Isa. 29:13). What will it take for wallpaper worship to fade away and be replaced with the real thing?

The bottom line is this: What are we doing with His house? Why are we settling for wallpaper worship?

I believe there is a new movement coming that will transform the body of Christ and change how we view and do worship. No one knows where it will come from or what the surrounding context of its coming will be. But I believe it is coming. As can be seen in the history of church movements, it will most likely come from outside the church. Wallpaper worship is historically cyclical. It thrives in times of great prosperity and dies in seasons of persecution.

We who identify ourselves as God-worshippers need to be identified as a group of people who do *not* want the same thing as everyone else (like my famous hit-record-producer friend quipped). There is a frustration and discontent that is rumbling among the laity. It is very real. Make no mistake: When the bride is frustrated, the Bridegroom listens. It is a cry from the heart of sheep who long to be led by shepherds who truly care for the condition of their flock—shepherds who are humble and integrated, and understand how to lead their followers into an experience that is transcendent and transformational. We must be willing to throw out anything that is not leading people into a life-changing worship experience that is fully participatory. Anything less is wallpaper worship.

Wallpaper worship does not encourage or allow participation. It is disconnected from its heritage, and proudly prances about as if to say, "Look at me. I know what the people want and I'll give it to them." It lacks the power of the Spirit because it confuses form with function. Once we experience true worship, we will quickly recognize wallpaper worship for what it is: the imposter of spirit and truth. Martin Luther recognized it. The Wesley brothers recognized it. The hippies who found Jesus on the beaches of Southern California recognized it. The bride of Christ is recognizing it again.

I encourage believers everywhere to become aware, look at what's happening, and acknowledge if you have become accepting of complacency. Like the people during the prophet Haggai's time, we are being called to rebuild a temple whose "latter glory . . . shall be greater than the former" (Hag. 2:9). If this message resonates with you, leave wallpaper worship behind, and seek a group of Christians who are high on participation and low on observation. Some have already left the glitz for historic liturgy. Some are walking out of the mainstream social-gospel churches for churches that espouse solid Bible teaching. Others are leaving megachurch productions for house churches. Form does not matter. According to the John 4 conversation, it never did.

Ultimately, our destiny as worshippers of almighty God lies with the One we worship. And the God we worship draws near to us when we worship Him the way He desires to be worshipped—in spirit and in truth. Remember the words of Jesus: "The hour is coming, and is now here, when the true worshippers will worship the Father in spirit and truth, for the Father is seeking such people to worship him" (John 4:23). The reality is we have no control whatsoever over how long we will live on this side of eternity. None. We are to be walking by faith and not by sight. If we are walking by faith, we can be at peace knowing that our destiny is in His hands.

So relax. If you are in church leadership, stop trying to build the next big worship ministry, thinking that if you mimic a certain style of worship you'll get the same results. If you are a churchgoer, a new believer, or a seasoned believer, you can stop praying for God to change your heart so that you can somehow accept wallpaper worship. You don't have to accept it. If God's not in it, why should you? So sing. Let others sing. Recite. Reflect. Participate. Demand to be allowed to participate. Live. Breathe. Worship.

> "It was for freedom that Christ set us free; therefore keep standing firm and do not be subject again to a yoke of slavery." (Gal. 5:1, NASB)

APPENDIX A

A HISTORICAL SURVEY OF

CHRISTIAN SONG

TIME OF CHRIST

Worship in the first and second centuries was characterized by much persecution, meeting in secret, and not much music.

170–220–Clement of Alexandria, "Father of Greek Theology," was the head of the school of catechism in Alexandria. His hymns reveal a marriage of Greek poetry and Christian truth. Some are still in use in the Greek Orthodox Church today.

313–With the Edict of Milan, Constantine made Christianity the religion of the Roman Empire, and music emerged as a joyous expression of freedom through psalm chanting and hymnwriting from personal experience.

330–The Roman Empire was moved to Byzantium and renamed Constantinople, which marked a division in the eastern and western empire (in their cultures and, eventually, in their worship styles). Latin replaced Greek as the language of the Western church and became universal by the sixth century. Antiphonal singing was introduced at Antioch and chanting of psalm verses became the responsibility of the congregation. In Antioch, hymn texts in verse form were introduced. Ephraim (AD 373), the foremost Syrian hymnwriter, employed popular tunes of heretical groups and substituted orthodox texts for people to sing.

364–The Council of Laodicea prohibited participation by the congregation and the use of instruments in worship. Only psalms and Scriptures could be sung. This accounts for the absence of hymns of personal experience from this time until six hundred years later.

CANON XV

374–397–Bishop Ambrose of Milan spread the antiphonal singing through his hymns. Choirs of boys and men would sing antiphonally, and then invite the congregation to participate. This is seen in the Western church. Ambrose wrote many hymns and influenced many others in the fourth century, like Augustine and Paulus ("Of the Father's Love Begotten"). Meanwhile, Roman liturgy was being developed as early as the first century. By the time of Gregory (AD 590–604), "Kyrie Eleison," "Gloria in Excelsis," and "Sanctus" were sung. The "Gloria Patri," added to each psalm sung in the service, was known in its present form by the end of the fourth century in both Eastern and Western churches; the "Te Deum laudamus" by the fifth century, "Credo" (used as a faith statement to unify the people) was added in the sixth century, and "Agnus Dei" was added in the seventh century, which is finally when the order of the Mass was standardized. These early expressions of praise and worship remain today in Roman Mass and are found, in part, in the Anglican, Episopal, and Lutheran churches.

7TH CENTURY

The melodies of the Roman chant were gathered together in a recognized repertoire. While this collection had no doubt begun earlier, it is generally attributed to Pope Gregory I (AD 590–6). With few additions, these chants remain the body of plainsong used by the Catholics today. Also known as Gregorian chant, a plainsong is monophonic, unaccompanied, and has no meter, with freedom of rhythm to fit the text. Examples of plainsongs used in today's Western Christian church: "Divinum Mysterium" and "O Come, O Come, Emmanuel." So strong was the influence of plainsong that it became the accepted pattern for Western churches. Before the end of the seventh century it reached England.

8TH CENTURY

Plainsong was taken to Germany.

9TH CENTURY

The church prospered under the reign of Charlemagne. Schools, churches, and monasteries were established across Europe. Christian songwriting flourished. Theodulph, a counselor of Charlemagne, wrote "All Glory, Laud and Honor." Other notable songs of this century: "Be Thou My Vision" and "O Come, O Come, Emmanuel." Secular Music: Minnesingers, meistersingers, trouveres, and troubadours of Germany,

England, and France. Nine hundred different forms of meters and stanzas were found in these songs, primarily from the twelfth through the sixteenth centuries. These did have an influence on Christian songwriting, as later we see a romantic character in choral song, as opposed to the strict classic restraint of Gregorian chant and early hymnwriting.

16TH CENTURY

The Italian Renaissance was heightening. Polyphonic music was *in*. Major and minor tonality was emerging. Music was being printed, as opposed to laboriously copied.

1529– Martin Luther wrote "A Mighty Fortress." The Reformation spurred scores of hymnwriters, and the first hymnals were published—which circulated the music all over Europe. Luther's passion to translate the Bible into the vernacular was doubled by his desire to have congregational song in the language of the common man so that all could lift their voices in praise to God (a radical idea).[1]

In spite of Luther's concern and desire for congregational singing and his efforts in writing and publishing hymns, congregational singing caught on very slowly. It wasn't until the last of the sixteenth century that hymn singing gained great prominence.

Meanwhile, John Calvin's influences were beginning to be felt as well in the latter sixteenth century. His services were dignified yet simple and consisted of prayer, preaching, and singing. Calvinistic philosophy and theology focused on the Bible and centered on the sovereignty of God. His firm conviction that congregational singing should employ only the Psalms in the vernacular of the people excluded any hymns developed in the Lutheran tradition. Calvin's philosophy of music was "simplicity and modesty." This was best achieved, said Calvin, by the unaccompanied voice! (Here we go again!)

In Geneva, the *Genevan Psalter of 1562*, a book of metrical psalms, was published. Most well-known is the "Old 100th." John Day's Psalter, printed in 1562, was a combination of English/French melodies/Anglo-Genevan Psalter. After the persecution of Protestants by Queen Mary, English Protestants moved to Frankfurt and Geneva, with John Knox as their pastor. Knox returned to Scotland in 1550 and published his own psalter, which came to be known as the *Scottish Psalter*.

17TH CENTURY

Later in Europe, the Thirty Years' War (1618-1648) had a big influence on German hymnody. The hymns written during and after this difficult period (both religiously and politically) revealed a changing emphasis from the previously objective characteristics to a more subjective emphasis. The experience of the war, which tested and tried Christian faith and courage, resulted in a greater sense of dependency on God's providence and care. Devotion and individual self-consciousness are evident in the hymns of this period.

This subjective religious thought also developed during the seventeenth century and culminated in Pietism in the latter part of the century. The Pietistic movement began with Jakob Spencer in 1670. "Praise to the Lord the Almighty" was written during this movement. The influence of Pietism produced hymns of greater subjectivity—more personal and passionate in character than the early Lutheran hymns. In the seventeenth century, singing continued, although there was debate and pockets of controversy over the issue of hymn singing throughout England and elsewhere. John Bunyan, Benjamin Keach, and others fostered some of the debate in their churches. Bunyan ended up in jail for twelve years during this period, and wrote *Pilgrim's Progress* while incarcerated.

The most recognized music composer of the seventeenth century was Johann Sebastian Bach. He didn't bother much with hymnwriting for congregational involvement, but instead brought choral music and church instrumental music to new heights. The organ became the primary instrument, and the chorale became the means through which his polyphonic style was expressed. His contributions came at the height of the Baroque era, which started in Italy and spread throughout Europe. Even some of the hymns written during this period reflected the Italian operatic style of singing.

18TH CENTURY

Because of the influence of the Baroque period, congregational singing eventually declined in the eighteenth century. Stalwart hymns of praise to God gave way to words of personal piety and individual expression. The organ became the prominent instrument as the skills of organists increased. Ornamental interludes between stanzas and excessive alteration of the hymn tunes proved detrimental to congregational singing.

19TH CENTURY

Most prominent hymnwriters were English, Isaac Watts being the best known. His philosophy was that the songs of the New Testament church should express the gospel of the

New Tesatament, whether in psalm versions or in freely composed hymns. He was also persuaded that Christian songs should not be forced to maintain the Calvinistic standards of strict adherence to literal Scripture, and he freely composed expressions of praise and devotion. Also, he held that Christian songs should express the thoughts and feelings of those who sang, rather than merely relate the experiences of the psalm writers of the Old Testament. "When I Survey," "Alas and Did My Savior Bleed," and "We Sing the Greatness of Our God" were first published in 1707. Later came, "O God Our Help in Ages Past," "Jesus Shall Reign Wherer the Sun," and "Joy to the World." Watts is known as the "Father of English Hymnody." He also wrote around the church calendar and each Sunday's sermon, so as to make his work relevant. Watts wrote sixty-five hundred hymns.

Simultaneously, Charles and John Wesley were writing as well. John was the founder of the Methodist movement. In his lifetime, Charles wrote more than sixty-five hundred hymns, and John wrote over two thousand. "And Can It Be That I Should Gain," "O For a Thousand Tongues to Sing," "Love Divine All Love's Excelling," and "Come, Thou Long Expected Jesus" are some of the best-known hymns. Around 1780, John Newton wrote "Glorious Things of Thee Are Spoken" and "Amazing Grace How Sweet the Sound."[2]

19TH CENTURY AMERICA

In the mid 1800s the hymn form was virtually abandoned in America for a more folk style song that included a refrain (start of the over and over and over again!) The language was common, as opposed to the loftier language found in older hymns, and words were more personal rather than theological. Musically, they were not written in poetic metered form as the hymns of old, but rather written with stanzas that were answered with an easy-to-remember refrain (or chorus) that was usually sung by the congregation (or the title was repeated throughout the text). It was more akin to the old English carols, which were folk in nature. They appealed to the masses, especially in revival meetings, which were the result of a new wave of revivalism starting around 1857. This period was known as the Second Great Awakening, and this music style became known as the gospel song. Examples: "What a Friend We Have in Jesus," "He Leadeth Me, O Blessed Thought," "Jesus Keep Me Near the Cross," "Trust and Obey," "I Need Thee Every Hour," "Just a Closer Walk with Thee."

Many of these songs became famous through the Moody/Sankey revivals of the 1870s and were published and sold at these meetings. Dwight L. Moody opened the Moody Bible Institute in Chicago in 1890. There, young pastors, evangelists, and song leaders were trained in the Moody/Ira Sankey styles of evangelism; and their influence, both musically and methodically, is still felt today. The Billy Graham Crusades of the next century were patterned after Moody.

Fanny Crosby was by far the most prolific gospel songwriter of the 1800s. Her songwriting continued at a phenomenal pace until shortly before her death in 1915 at the age of ninety-five. She wrote over eight thousand hymns and gospel songs. Most of her life was spent in New York City as a member of St Johns Methodist/Episcopal Church. Some of her songs include "To God Be the Glory," "All the Way My Savior Leads Me," "Jesus Keep Me Near the Cross," "Pass Me Not, O Gentle Savior."

Negro spirituals from the seventeenth, eighteenth, and nineteenth centuries are a rich heritage of songs that have crept into predominantly white church repertoires. Many of these songs were used as "code" in the cotton fields and included chanting that was African in nature and rhythm. Christianity spread quickly among the slaves because they related to Israel's plight of being in captivity in Egypt and under Roman rule. To dream about a mansion in glory was a great source of hope to enslaved Africans, who were separated from their families and, in many cases, not allowed to meet together except for church. For black slaves and their families, the worship service became all they had in the way of public community meetings. Even though these were a poor and uneducated people in nineteenth-century America, what a rich repertoire of songs emerged—with a simple yet profound theology born from the cotton fields of the South.

Among the thousands of negro spirituals are "Swing Low, Sweet Chariot," "Let Us Break Bread Together," "Go, Tell It on the Mountain," "Lord, I Want to Be a Christian," "There Is a Balm in Gilead," and "Were You There When They Crucified My Lord?"

20TH CENTURY

The twentieth century saw the Pentecostal movement of the 1920s ("Turn Your Eyes Upon Jesus"), two world wars, great prosperity, the advent of rock and roll and its infiltration into church music, and the Jesus movement's folk style of the 1960s and '70s. It gave birth to contemporary Christian music. Song recording and publishing exploded and the praise chorus took hold (Integrity Music). In England, once again, writers such as Graham Kendrick and Martin Smith stood at the apex of a young church movement, with modern songs of praise at the center (Hillsong, Australia and Jesus Culture, USA).

21ST CENTURY

As we move forward in the twenty-first century, which songs will remain? No one knows—and we won't know until we reach heaven and look down to see and hear what the saints are singing. But it is clear that the musical forms of the past, that have lasted since the beginning of Christianity, are still a force in today's worship, both Protestant and Catholic. That is why we need to be exposed to as many legitimate forms of worship as possible—so that we can pass on the legacy of worship and the legacy of hymns that belong exclusively to us, the church.[3]

APPENDIX B

CHURCH CALENDAR FOR DUMMIES

THE CHRISTMAS CYCLE

ADVENT SEASON

Advent means "something is coming." It is the time of anticipation of the coming of Christ in the form of a baby, born to the Virgin Mary. There are four Sundays in Advent, the first being the first Sunday following Thanksgiving, and the fourth being the Sunday prior to Christmas.

Most churches celebrate Advent with an Advent wreath. The wreath consists of four candles in the circular portion and a fifth in the middle. Each Sunday a candle is lit to represent the prophecy, the manger, the shepherds, the angels, and, finally, the Christ child. His candle is lit on Christmas Eve.

Appropriate hymns: "O Come, O Come, Emmanuel," "Come, Thou Long Expected Jesus," "Of the Father's Love Begotten."

CHRISTMAS SEASON

Christmas begins on December 24, with celebration lasting through December 26.

EPIPHANY SEASON

Epiphany means "light." It literally is the celebration of the star that led the wise men to Bethlehem and told the world that the Savior had come. There are eight Sundays in Epiphany, all celebrating light in the Lord's life: His baptism, transfiguration, etc. The last Sunday after Epiphany leads into Lent. Most evangelical churches that celebrate Epiphany only do so one Sunday in January, emphasizing the gifts of the Magi and the star.

Appropriate hymns: "We Three Kings of Orient Are," "Break Forth, O Beauteous Heavenly Light."

THE EASTER CYCLE

SEASON OF LENT

Lent is a forty-day season of cleansing, to prepare for Christ's suffering and death. It begins on Ash Wednesday, moves through six Sundays (the sixth being Palm Sunday), and culminates in Holy Week. Many believers fast from a particular food (sugar, starches, coffee) or a particular activity (movies, entertainment) during this season. The idea is to cleanse the body, mind, and spirit in preparation for Holy Week and our Lord's passion and crucifixion.

HOLY WEEK

This week is the most prominent of all Christian holidays. It begins with Palm Sunday, Maundy Thursday (recognition of the Last Supper), and Good Friday (the recognition of the suffering and death of Christ). It culminates with Easter Sunday and the celebration of the resurrection of Christ.

THANKSGIVING:

A REASON TO WORSHIP & BE THANKFUL – TO LEAD OTHERS . . . .

Uniquely American and Christian

Use *The Light and the Glory* to do readings with responsive hymns & choruses[1]

Extremely meaningful for American Christians

APPENDIX C

THE CREEDS

THE NICENE CREED

I believe in one God, the Father Almighty, Maker of heaven and earth, and of all things visible and invisible.

And in one Lord Jesus Christ, the only-begotten Son of God, begotten of the Father before all worlds; God of God, Light of Light, very God of very God; begotten, not made, being of one substance with the Father, by whom all things were made.

Who, for us men for our salvation, came down from heaven, and was incarnate by the Holy Spirit of the virgin Mary, and was made man; and was crucified also for us under Pontius Pilate; He suffered and was buried; and the third day He rose again, according to the Scriptures; and ascended into heaven, and sits on the right hand of the Father; and He shall come again, with glory, to judge the living and the dead; whose kingdom shall have no end.

And I believe in the Holy Ghost, the Lord and Giver of Life; who proceeds from the Father; who with the Father and the Son together is worshipped and glorified; who spoke by the prophets.

And I believe one holy catholic and apostolic Church. I acknowledge one baptism for the remission of sins; and I look for the resurrection of the dead, and the life of the world to come. Amen.

THE APOSTLES' CREED

I believe in God, the Father Almighty,
Maker of heaven and earth;
and in Jesus Christ his only Son, our Lord;
who was conceived by the Holy Spirit,
born of the Virgin Mary,
suffered under Pontius Pilate,
was crucified, dead, and buried;
the third day he rose from the dead;
he ascended into heaven,
and is seated at the right hand of God the Father Almighty;
from thence he shall come to judge the living and the dead.
I believe in the Holy Spirit,
the holy Christian church,
the communion of saints,
the forgiveness of sins,
the resurrection of the body,
and the life everlasting.
Amen.

A NEW CREED
VMI DECLARATION OF FAITH
(FROM VIRGINIA MILITARY INSTITUTE CHAPEL, LEXINGTON, VA)

I believe that in the beginning was the Word and the Word was with God and the Word was God; that the Word became flesh and dwelt among us. I believe that the fullness of God existed in the person of Christ; that Jesus was the image of the invisible God; that He was made in the likeness of His brethren in all things; that He was tempted in all things as we are, yet He was without sin. I believe that Jesus laid down His life for my sake; that no one took His life from Him but that of His own choice, He laid it down. I believe that the Just One died for the unjust that He might bring me to God; that He bore my sin in His body on the tree; that He was condemned and forsaken in my place; that the wrath of God came upon Him for my sin, and that His death paid the consequence for my judgment. I believe Jesus Christ is the Son of God, that He rose from the dead; that He appeared to witnesses in demonstration of His power over sin, death and the grave. I believe that faith alone secures me in right relationship with the Creator, God, and because of faith in Christ I have been given the right to be a child of God and can call Him my Father and my God. Amen.

APPENDIX D

US AIR FORCE HYMN

Lord, Guard and Guide the Men Who Fly
By Mary C.D. Hamilton

Lord, guard and guide the men who fly
Through the great spaces of the sky;
Be with them traversing the air
In darkening storms or sunshine fair.
Thou who dost keep with tender might
The balanced birds in all their flight,
Thou of the tempered winds, be near,
That, having thee, they know no fear.
Control their minds with instinct fit
What time, adventuring, they quit
The firm security of land;
Grant steadfast eye and skillful hand.
Aloft in solitudes of space,
Uphold them with Thy saving grace.
O God, protect the men who fly
Thro' lonely ways beneath the sky.

APPENDIX E

THE LARRY NORMAN STORY

The Impact of a Song and the Danger of Not Knowing
What Came Prior on Platform

I was attending the Christian Artists Seminar in Estes Park, Colorado in the summer of 1986. It was a time of transition for what became known as contemporary Christian music. It seemed surreal to watch artists and writers who got their initial start during the Jesus movement, over a decade later, being promoted commercially by a few privately owned Christian record companies. The contemporary Christian music business was becoming a viable alternative genre. With Christian artists successfully selling around three hundred thousand units (in the secular side of the music business three hundred thousand would get an artist dropped from the label), we felt we finally had commercial viability.

During the music business seminar at Estes Park, an original artist from the Jesus movement was being featured in the evening concert showcase segment of the week. It was Larry

Norman. Norman had always been considered counterculture, with his screaming high tenor voice, his long straight white/blonde hair that draped over his shoulders, and his Southern California blue jeans and T-shirts that he wore to church. But it was not just his appearance that many in the church thought edgy. His lyrics were always crafted from a street-talk style which he brought into his Christian experience from his Southern California culture. Most artists from a worldly past will change over time and start sounding more religiously respectable. Not Larry. His lyrics were some of the most profound, straightforward lyrics out there. Since much of the theology expressed during the Jesus movement was apocalyptic, Larry's songs fit in well (e.g., "I Wish We'd All Been Ready"). In church circles, he was considered a prophet by some and a heretic by others.

Larry and his band took to the stage at the YMCA of the Rockies to perform a song he had written entitled "Messiah." The song portrayed the battle of Armageddon during the end of time, where all the armies of the earth would converge on Israel to destroy her. The climax of the song was loud, huge, and confusing, complete with backup singers, drums, brass section, and electric guitars—all playing in such a frenzy as to represent the battle itself. Finally, Larry screamed over the music at the top of his voice, "Messiah! Messiah! Where are You, Messiah?!" He was portraying Israel calling for salvation from the battle.

The audience rose to their feet. People were crying, tears streaming down their faces. Many were yelling with Larry, "Messiah, Messiah!" Suddenly, the song was over and the band left the stage, but the audience was still crying out and wouldn't let Larry leave. Amid the audience noise, Larry came back on stage and in typical form told the audience that the program was on a time restraint and he had been told to leave the stage. The place came unglued! Some people were protesting, some were praising God, some were still grieving for Israel, and others were still yelling "Messiah!"—while others stood there in shocked silence.

A popular author of the day, who had spoken earlier in the week, immediately got on stage, took the mic from Larry and made a statement that what was happening in that moment was real and not programmed or planned. He proclaimed it to be the power of God's presence and His anointing in music. After the author read a passage from Isaiah, something unprecedented happened. Suddenly, the man yelled into the mic, "Damn commerciality! We don't need commerciality when God is wanting to pour out His spirit through our music. Damn commerciality!"

The already ramped-up crowd went through the roof! Everything that wasn't nailed down came loose. Yelling, screaming, jumping, arms flailing, record company executives angry and leaving. It was bedlam. The master of ceremonies then took over the microphone, attempting to calm down the audience. The emcee stuck to his agenda, as there were more artists slated for the evening's showcase that needed their time. While many in the audience were still standing, the emcee introduced the next act. The next singer took the stage with a digital keyboard on a stand, some preproduced tracks he would cue with a button, and a comedic style a la Weird Al Yankovic. He had no connection with what had just happened or how this audience was feeling. Apparently he had just arrived backstage and had no knowledge of what his audience had just experienced with Larry Norman. As he pranced about the stage, trying to be funny and cute, half the audience walked out. They were still being affected by Larry Norman's "Messiah." I have never, before or since, seen anything that powerful transpire from the performance of one song.

APPENDIX F

DEVOTIONAL SONGS

Songs of devotion contain highly subjective and personally intimate phrases and words, as opposed to songs that declare, which talk of God's attributes, His kingdom, His works, His loftiness, His grandeur. Songs of devotion express the very personal feelings, experiences, and sentiments of their writers. The following are examples. Note the personal language and expression. Note the use of the words *I, my, me,* etc.

BE THOU MY VISION

Be Thou *my* vision, O Lord of *my* heart;
Naught be all else to *me*, save that Thou art;
Thou *my* best thought, by day or by night,
Waking or sleeping, Thy presence *my* light.

Be Thou *my* wisdom, and Thou *my* true word;
I ever with Thee and Thou with *me*, Lord.

Thou *my* great Father, and *I* Thy true son;
Thou in *me* dwelling, and *I* with Thee one.

Riches *I* heed not, nor man's empty praise,
Thou *mine* inheritance, now and always:
Thou and Thou only, first in *my* heart,
High King of Heaven, *my* treasure Thou art.

High King of heaven, *my* victory won,
May *I* reach heaven's joys, O bright heaven's sun!
Heart of *my* own heart, whatever befall,
Still be *my* vision, O Ruler of all.

IT IS WELL WITH MY SOUL

When peace like a river attendeth my way,
When sorrows like sea billows roll;
Whatever my lot, Thou hast taught me to say,
"It is well, it is well with my soul."

Though Satan should buffet, though trials should come,
Let this blest assurance control:
That Christ has regarded my helpless estate,
And has shed His own blood for my soul.

My sin—Oh, the bliss of this glorious thought!—
My sin, not in part, but the whole,
Is nailed to the cross, and I bear it no more;
Praise the Lord! Praise the Lord, O my soul!

TAKE MY LIFE AND LET IT BE

Take my life, and let it be
Consecrated, Lord, to Thee.
Take my moments and my days,
Let them flow in ceaseless praise,
Let them flow in ceaseless praise.

Take my voice and let me sing
Always, only for my King.
Take my lips, and let them be
Filled with messages from Thee,
Filled with messages from Thee.

Take my love, my Lord, I pour
At Thy feet its treasure store;
Take myself, and I will be
Ever, only, all for Thee,
Ever, only, all for Thee.

AMAZING GRACE

Amazing grace—how sweet the sound—
That saved a wretch like me!
I once was lost but now am found,
Was blind but now I see.

'Twas grace that taught my heart to fear,
And grace my fears relieved;
How precious did that grace appear
The hour I first believed!

Through many dangers, toils, and snares
I have already come;
'Tis grace hath brought me safe thus far,
And grace will lead me home.

NOTES

Introduction: This Is a Football

1. David Maraniss, *When Pride Still Mattered: A Life Of Vince Lombardi* (New York: Simon & Schuster, 2000), 274.

Chapter 1: Worship: A Major Award

1. *A Christmas Story*, directed by Bob Clark (Los Angeles: MGM/UA Entertainment Co., 1983).

2. Alan Jay Lerner, lyricist, and Frederick Loewe, composer, "Why Can't the English?," *My Fair Lady*, Milwaukee: Hal Leonard, 1956.

3. Elmer L. Towns and Vernon M. Whaley, *Worship through the Ages: How the Great Awakenings Shape Evangelical Worship* (Nashville: B&H Publishing, 2012), 253.

4. Rachel Held Evans, "Want Millennials Back in the Pews? Stop Trying to Make Church 'Cool,'" *Washington Post*, April 30, 2015, https://www.washingtonpost.com/opinions/jesus-doesnt-tweet/2015/04/30/fb07ef1a-ed01-11e4-8666-a1d756d0218e_story.html.

Chapter 2: The Worship Conversation

1. Gary Thomas, *Sacred Marriage:What If God Designed Marriage to Make Us Holy More Than to Make Us Happy?* (Grand Rapids: Zondervan, 2000), 58; Leon Morris, *The Gospel According to John*, New International Commentary on the New Testament (Grand Rapids: Wm. B. Eerdmans Publishing Co., 1971), 274.

2. Matthew Henry, *Matthew Henry's Commentary on the Whole Bible*, vol. 5, *Matthew to John* (Hendrickson Publishers, 1991, 2006), 726.

Chapter 3: Worship Is Our Heritage

1. Bill Senyard, "Zechariah and Worship," December 24, 2013, Lookout Mountain Community Church, Golden, CO.

2. John Kander, composer, and Fred Ebb, lyricist, "Razzle Dazzle," *Chicago the Musical* (New York: Samuel French, 1975).

3. Ray C. Stedman, "The 400 Years Between the Old and New Testaments," RayStedman.org, 1995, accessed November 27, 2017, https://www.raystedman.org/bible-overview/adventuring/the-400-years-between-the-old-and-new-testaments.

4. A.W. Tozer, *Whatever Happened to Worship?: A Call to True Worship* (Camp Hill, PA: Wingspread Publishers, 1985), 34.

5. Robert E. Webber, *Worship Is a Verb: Celebrating God's Mighty Deeds of Salvation* (Waco: Word Books, 1985), 43.

6. Webber, *Worship Is a Verb*. 44.

Chapter 4: Worship Is Our Privilege

1. James M. McPherson, *Battle Cry of Freedom: The Civil War Era* (Oxford: Oxford University Press, 1988).

2. Joseph M. Scriven, "What a Friend We Have in Jesus" (1855), Timeless Truths Free Online Library, accessed January 16, 2018,

http://library.timelesstruths.org/music/What_a_Friend_We_
Have_in_Jesus/.

3. "Blessed Be Your Name," by Matt Redman and Beth Redman,
   track 2 on *Where Angels Fear to Tread*, ThankYou Music, 2002.

4. Harvey Schmidt, composer, and Tom Jones, lyricist, "Try to
   Remember," *The Fantasticks*, Milwaukee: Hal Leonard, 1960.

5. Gary Thomas, *Sacred Marriage: What If God Designed Marriage
   to Make Us Holy More Than to Make Us Happy?* (Grand Rapids:
   Zondervan, 2000), 129.

6. "What Is Worship? Thoughts from Wimber," VineyardUSA,
   accessed January 16, 2018, https://vineyardusa.org/library/
   what-is-worship-thoughts-from-wimber/.

7. Roland H. Bainton, *Here I Stand: A Life of Martin Luther* (Nashville: Abingdon Press, 1978), 190.

8. Roland H. Bainton, *Here I Stand*, 190.

9. Roger J. Green, "1738 John & Charles Wesley Experience
   Conversions," Christian History Institute, accessed at Chris-
   tianHistoryInstitute.org, November 27, 2017, https://chris-
   tianhistoryinstitute.org/magazine/article/john-and-charles-
   converted.

10. Charles Wesley, "O for a Thousand Tongues to Sing" (1739),
    Hymnary.org, accessed January 17, 2018, https://hymnary.org/
    text/o_for_a_thousand_tongues_to_sing_my.

11. Anne Ortlund, *Up with Worship: How to Quit Playing Church*
    (Nashville: B&H Publishing, 2001), 38.

Chapter 6: Worship Isn't Casual

1. Rick Warren, *The Purpose Driven Life* (Grand Rapids: Zondervan, 2002), 77.

2. Don Chapman, "Why Rock Star Worship Leaders Are Getting

Fired," *Worship Leader*, February 1, 2016, http://churchleaders.com/worship/worship-articles/170929-don-chapman-rock-star-worship-leaders-are-getting-fired.html.

3. A.W. Tozer, *Whatever Happened to Worship?: A Call to True Worship* (Camp Hill, PA: WingSpread Publishers, 2012).

Chapter 8: Worship Isn't Music

1. *Amadeus*, directed by Milos Foreman (Los Angeles: Orion Pictures, 1984), film.

Chapter 9: Three Things Missed in Traditional Worship

1. Jeri Watson, "The '60s Become a Time of Social Revolution and Unrest," Voice of America, 2007, http://www.manythings.org/voa/history/214.html.

2. Mary C.D. Hamilton, "Lord, Guard And Guide The Men Who Fly" (1915), Hymnary.org, accessed February 6, 2018, https://hymnary.org/text/lord_guard_and_guide_the_men_who_fly.

3. William J. Reynolds, *A Survey of Christian Hymnody* (New York: Holt, Reinhart & Winston, Inc., 1963), 7.

4. Madeleine L'Engle, *Walking On Water: Reflections on Faith and Art* (Wheaton, IL: Harold Shaw Publishers, 1998), 183.

5. Reynolds, *A Survey of Christian Hymnody*, 11.

6. Michael Lipka, "Mainline Protestants make up shrinking number of U.S. adults," Pew Research Center, May 18, 2015, http://www.pewresearch.org/fact-tank/2015/05/18/mainline-protestants-make-up-shrinking-number-of-u-s-adults/.

7. Jaroslav Pelikan, *The Vindication of Tradition: The 1983 Jefferson Lecture in the Humanities* (New Haven, CT: Yale University, 1984), 65.

Chapter 10: Three Things Missed in Contemporary Worship

1. "The Times They Are a-Changin'," Bob Dylan, track 1 on *The Times They Are a-Changin'*, Columbia, 1964.
2. "Revelation Song," Jennie Lee Riddle, track 9 on *Glorious* by Christ for the Nations Institute, Gateway Create Publishing (Capitol CMG Publishing), 2004, compact disc.
3. Nicene Creed, Christian Classics Ethereal Library, accessed November 28, 2017, https://www.ccel.org/creeds/nicene.creed.html.
4. Frank E. Gaebelein, *The Christian, the Arts, and Truth: Regaining the Vision of Greatness*, ed. D. Bruce Lockerbie (Multnomah, OR: Multnomah Press, 1985), 88.
5. Rachel Held Evans, "Want Millennials Back in the Pews? Stop Trying to Make Church 'Cool,'" *Washington Post*, April 30, 2015, https://www.washingtonpost.com/opinions/jesus-doesnt-tweet/2015/04/30/fb07ef1a-ed01-11e4-8666-a1d756d0218e_story.html.

Chapter 11: Three Principles of Planning: Participation, (un)Predictability, Power

1. Recently, I was booked to lead music for a denominational conference. Prior to starting, as I was tuning my guitar, one of the speakers for the event came to the stage to set up his computer at the podium. I said, "Hi. My name's Danny." He responded, "Are you one of the presenters or the musician?" I thought, *What an interesting question. Is the assumption that as a musician I have nothing to present other than a little music to get people in the door so we can start the "real" part of the program?* There are low expectations of musicians involved in worship. In some cases, those low expectations have been well earned.

2. I call this "Pre-Reformation Worship." Whenever this cycle has occurred there is a movement that comes along and changes how the church worships. These cycles used to run hundreds of years apart. Now they run about every twenty-five to thirty years. We are currently primed for a new movement that will bring a new cycle in how the church worships.

3. John Cleese, "Unbound: John Cleese in conversation with John Hodgman (full talk)," interview by John Hodgman, published by BAM.org, November 5, 2014, https://www.youtube.com/watch?v=nL0dmBy5qTw.

4. Linda Ronstadt, "Linda Ronstadt on Parkinson's Diagnosis: Life Is 'Different,'" interview by Robin Roberts, *Good Morning America*, published by ABC News, September 16, 2013, https://www.youtube.com/watch?v=sBHJL_splYg.

5. Pastors should note: If your musicians are playing all new songs all the time, your flock is not participating because they are not being *allowed* to participate.

6. Chapman, "Why Rock Star Worship Leaders Are Getting Fired."

7. Christian radio is a *source* for new music, but not the *standard* by which corporate worship music effectiveness is measured. I encourage church musicians to write their own songs, and to encourage congregants to write new songs from their own experiences in their local body. This is where much of the Vineyard music came from. Many classic Vineyard songs of the 1980s and '90s were born out of sermons and relevant experiences. The Vineyard repertoire is still in use as it stands the test of time and scriptural accuracy.

8. Hymn lyrics *are* the hymns. The melodies were often interchanged with lyrics that matched their syllabic rhythms. I maintain that the reason so many hymns from the English and German hymnody

catalogs are so articulate is that the European hymnwriters of the sixteenth, seventeenth, eighteenth, and nineteenth centuries had a firm grasp of language, grammar, and usage. This was because they were educated by reading the classics—Plato, Greek mythologies, the Bible—and the books of the eighteenth and nineteenth centuries, such as Keats and Milton. Lyrics such as "Long my imprisoned spirit lay / Fast bound in sin and nature's night; / Thine eye diffused a quickening ray, / I woke, the dungeon flamed with light; / My chains fell off, my heart was free; / I rose, went forth and followed Thee," written by Charles Wesley around 1770, are reflective of English language not founded in colloquialism, nor matched today by writers like myself who were raised in popular culture and babysat by television programming.

9. Until the late 1990s, churches were notorious for inadequate sound—typically a public address system which was designed for a speaker behind a lectern. In larger church settings one might find choir mics, flown from the rafters. Modern music gear such as vocal mics, direct boxes, amps, or drum kits were not available in most churches until the 1990s. This has always been a mystery to me since the contemporary style of music has been active in Protestant worship since the Jesus movement of the early 1970s, and in the Catholic folk mass since the mid-1960s.

Chapter 12: Three Essentials of Evaluation: Declare, Respond, Devotion

1. Charles Wesley, "And Can It Be That I Should Gain" (1738), Hymnary.org, accessed February 14, 2018, https://hymnary.org/text/and_can_it_be_that_i_should_gain.

2. William J. Reynolds, *A Survey of Christian Hymnody* (New York: Holt, Reinhart & Winston, Inc., 1963), 22.

3. Martin Luther, "A Mighty Fortress Is Our God" (1529), Hymnary.org, accessed February 16, 2018, https://hymnary.org/text/a_mighty_fortress_is_our_god_a_bulwark.

Appendix A: A Historical Survey of Christian Song

1. John Fines, *Who's Who in the Middle Ages*.
2. Donald Jay Grout, *A History of Western Music*.
3. Reynolds, A Survey of Christian Hymnody.

Appendix B: Church Calendar for Dummies

1. Peter Marshall and David Manuel, *The Light and the Glory* (Ada, MI: Revell, 2009).

PUBLICATIONS

Fort Washington, PA 19034

This book is published by CLC Publications, an outreach
of CLC Ministries International. The purpose of CLC is to
make evangelical Christian literature available to all nations
so that people may come to faith and maturity in the Lord
Jesus Christ. We hope this book has been life changing and
has enriched your walk with God through the work of the
Holy Spirit. If you would like to know more about CLC,
we invite you to visit our website:

www.clcusa.org

To know more about the remarkable story of the founding of
CLC International we encourage you to read

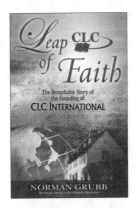

LEAP OF FAITH

Norman Grubb

Paperback

Size 5¹/₄ x 8, Pages 248

ISBN: 978-0-87508-650-7

ISBN (*e-book*): 978-1-61958-055-8

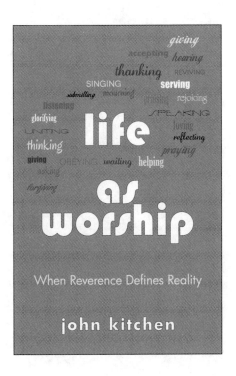

LIFE AS WORSHIP

John Kitchen

Life as Worship explores the life and psalms of Asaph to understand what it means to live a life of worship. This study of Asaph's writings gives readers insight into the psalms' various applications to all seasons of life, including: thankfulness, mourning, reflection, faithfulness and revival.

Paperback
Size 5^1/$_4$ x 8, Pages 267
ISBN: 978-1-61958-162-3
ISBN (*e-book*): 978-1-61958-163-0

AMAZING LOVE

Corrie ten Boom

Following her miraculous release from a Nazi concentration camp, Corrie ten Boom refused to give in to the weakness of anger, claiming, "Forgiveness requires more strength than hatred." Sharing incredible stories of encounters with people from all walks of life, Corrie illustrates how a childlike faith in the wisdom and love of God pushes us to forgive the seemingly impossible.

Paperback
Size 5¹/₄ x 8, Pages 122
ISBN: 978-1-61958-288-0
ISBN (*e-book*): 978-1-61958-289-7

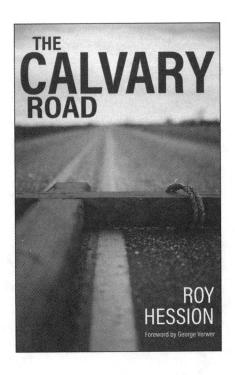

THE CALVARY ROAD

Roy Hession

Do you long for revival and power in your life? Learn how Jesus can fill you with His spirit through brokenness, repentance and confession in this updated version of Hession's classic, *The Calvary Road*. In the course of eleven chapters, Hession emphasizes the need for personal revival in life with Christ.

Paperback
Size 4^1/$_4$ x 7, Pages 162
ISBN: 978-1-61958-226-2
ISBN (*e-book*): 978-1-61958-227-9

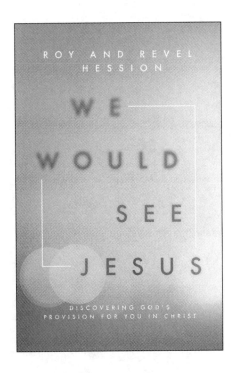

WE WOULD SEE JESUS

Roy and Revel Hession

In this classic companion to the best-selling book *The Calvary Road*, Roy and Revel Hession teach that seeing Jesus is the answer to every aspect of our Christian life. Painting a refreshing and challenging picture of the Lord Jesus, they tell of Him in whom all the needs of human hearts are met. Two themes occur again and again in these pages—grace and revival—but the main direction and theme is always Jesus.

Paperback
Size 4¹/₄ x 7, Pages 189
ISBN: 978-1-61958-266-8
ISBN (*e-book*): 978-1-61958-267-5